RITUAL
IN FAMILY LIVING

RITUAL
IN FAMILY LIVING,

A CONTEMPORARY STUDY

By JAMES H. S. BOSSARD

AND

ELEANOR S. BOLL

PHILADELPHIA
UNIVERSITY OF PENNSYLVANIA PRESS

Copyright 1950

UNIVERSITY OF PENNSYLVANIA PRESS

Manufactured in the United States of America

Published in Great Britain, India and Pakistan
by J. G. N. Brown: Oxford University Press
London, Bombay, and Karachi

To

ALICE CARTER DICKERMAN

In appreciation of continuing interest and encouragement

FOREWORD

This book has been eight years in the making. If the distance traversed seems short, the difficulties in the terrain must be obvious. We have been exploring virgin territory in which there were no signposts or even footpaths by pioneers. On first forays into the unexplored, one should not expect to find the finished highway.

With this claim for originality on the one hand, and apology for the imperfection of our work on the other, we launch this study, with hesitation and yet with confidence. We should like to think that this is an important book, not necessarily for its achievements, but for the vistas it may open, both in the study of the family and in the contemporary study of social origins. The study of social origins, be it noted, is not necessarily antediluvian.

As in many cases of joint authorship, the specific contributions of the respective authors cannot always be identified. Throughout the entire study, there has been constant exchange of ideas. It seems proper, however, to say that chapters 1, 2, 9, and 10 were written by Mr. Bossard, and chapters 3, 4, 5, 6, 7, and 8 were written wholly or largely by Mrs. Boll.

To the many persons who have contributed their own family rituals, we extend our sincerest thanks. Without their coöperation this study could not have been made. Professor Raymond Kennedy of Yale University, Professor Jessie Bernard of Pennsylvania State College, and Professor A. H. Hobbs of the University of Pennsylvania made suggestions which were incorporated into this volume. To Mrs. Winogene Pratt Sanger, Research Associate in the Carter Foundation, we are indebted for the technical preparation of the manuscript. Finally, acknowledgment is due to the William T. Carter Foundation of the University of Pennsylvania, which made this study possible.

JAMES H. S. BOSSARD

ELEANOR S. BOLL

September 8, 1949

Contents

custom

The Challenge of Contemporary Family Life

E AMERICANS are the most married people in the world. Our marriage rate is customarily the highest in the world. Similarly, in the proportion of the population fifteen years of age and over that is married, and in the percentage of those widowed and divorced who remarry, no other great nation compares with us. We marry relatively early in life, too, when comparisons are made with other peoples living in an advanced stage of culture; and the average age of marriage in this country has been falling steadily for decades. The median age of men marrying for the first time was almost two years lower in 1940 than in 1890; for women, the difference was about half of one year. In other words, we marry earlier and oftener than do peoples in other comparable cultures.

We marry with less reference to preparatory rituals and ceremonial features than other and older nations employ to conserve the sanctity of the marital rite. No one who studies modern marriage practices can fail to note how often life's most permanent and intimate obligations are assumed in the neon-lighted, cigarette-littered offices of commercial marriage performers, to the underlying strains of music that is neither sacred nor stirring. These are but the more glaring instances in the field of marriage of that growing lack of the ceremonial in American life, which so many people mistake for democracy, but which really is only cheap tawdriness.

No other nation has ever formally educated so large a proportion of its young people as we do, and formal courses in the field of marriage and family problems are an integral part of the American system of education. The 1,968 professors who give 657 such courses in 550 colleges and universities indicate the scope of this emphasis at the level of higher education. Courses in high schools, group instruction given by such agencies as the Young Men's and Young Women's Christian Association, and the organized efforts of many pastors in the church, supplement and extend the scope of education for marriage at other than the collegiate level.

We are the most divorced people in the world. In recent years the number of divorces has approximated one-third of the total number of marriages; in selected cities the number equals, and even exceeds, one-half of the total. Moreover, divorce is but one index of the larger problem of family disorganization. There are the other obvious forms of legal separation, desertion, and the mutual going of one's own way by the respective partners by tacit agreement. These, together with the many kinds of family tension in which the severance of relationships does not occur, amount to a percentage of marital failure that is both appalling and unparalleled.

The four groups of facts just cited are well known to students of family problems. They have been restated here so that they may be considered together, in their relationship to each other. Facts are important for the processes of rational thought, but it is when brought into relationship with other facts that their real meaning often comes to be revealed. Considered thus together, the above facts raise some very pointed questions about the contemporary family, the emphases in the current literature and educational programs dealing with it, and the insights which scientific students have and have not developed in the field of family behavior. Are American teaching methods at fault, or do the difficulties center chiefly in the teaching material that is available? How well do we really understand the nature, needs, and problems of family life? Has the literature on marriage and the family been developed to meet the favor of romantic youth, and subsequently been organized into a commercial market, or does it deal with problems inductively identified as important to the promotion of successful family living? How much have sociologists and other professional students of the family concerned themselves with the mechanics of family life or the factors in successful family operation, and to what extent have they pandered to popular questions which interest the romantically inclined of the moment? What are the factors which make a go out of family life? How can family solidarity be cemented as the years go by?

How the Current Literature on the Family Came to Develop

In seeking to answer these questions, it will be helpful to recall how the literature, sociological and otherwise, on the family came to develop as a part of the American educational program. This story constitutes a unique chapter in the history of our schools and colleges because of the very different way in which it came to be added to existing courses of instruction. Other courses in our educational program are devised invariably at the top, and by the top, and imposed from above upon the students. Subjects are taught customarily because educational leaders consider them essential to the education of an immature, and often reluctant, youth. Not so with courses on marriage and the family. They have sprung mostly from the "grass roots." In most instances, and particularly in the days of the beginnings of such educational experiments, it was the students who asked for them, often repeatedly and over a period of years, until a cautious and timid faculty finally decided to venture a few lectures or a semester course.

In answer to the demands of students, many different kinds of courses, and attendant course material such as books, articles, and research papers, have come into being. Naturally they reveal a variety of content, and of emphases too, but considered by and large, two motifs, if a musical term may be borrowed for the moment, have come to dominate. The first of these is the romantic motif. As presently interpreted, this means that you marry for love, and that you work at it after marriage. A successful marriage is the final realization of the romantic attraction; other kinds of marriage are but substitutes for the real thing. Much is made of marriage for love as evidence of progress in the field of marital relations. We no longer marry for convenience, to promote a career, to get a dowry, or to please our kinfolk, as people unhappily used to do, but to establish a personally desirable relationship which is voluntary rather than coercive, rests upon personal choice rather than family arrangement, and aims at individual happiness rather than personal advantage.

It will come as a surprise to many people to learn that this emphasis upon romantic attraction as the basis for marriage has not always existed. Not that romantic love is a new idea, for strong emotional attraction between individuals of opposite sex is obviously as old as the human heartbeat. What is new is the relative place accorded to romance in the family, and its final acceptance as the primary basis of marriage selection and maintenance. The romantic complex, as it is often called, came into our Western culture with the French troubadours of the twelfth and thirteenth centuries, and has reached its most exalted position in recent American literature and practice, until today it emerges as the accepted cornerstone of the marriage relationship. Taking a world-wide view, and considered in the retrospect of time, romance as the basis of marriage is a relatively new social experiment, still confined to a minority of the world's peoples. Like the romantic stories of the "pulp" magazines, it will be interesting to see "how it comes out."

Individualism is the second basis for modern marriage, as developed in the current literature on the family. That is to say, marriage is looked upon as a vehicle for the personality development of its contractors. A good marriage is one that contributes fully and freely to personality development; a poor marriage is one that hinders such development. This particular emphasis is, of course, but one phase of a much larger ideological pattern which is as distinctly American as ancestor worship has been typical of the Chinese. The early application and cultivation of this philosophy comes in our schools, where children are encouraged to be, and to express, themselves. In recent years, the stronger this emphasis in a school, the more "progressive" do we pronounce it to be. In marriage, this individualistic trend expresses itself in freedom of choice of mate, disregarding often the advice and admonition of parents, kinfolk, pastor, priest, or any of the traditional values and modes in mate selection. After marriage, this philosophy is maintained. From the beginning of their marriage, contemporary mates organize their lives, within limitations of course, on an individualistic basis; in many cases, as time goes on, these limitations are reduced in number and in extent to which they are honored. It is at this point that the esoteric speak of personal schematization within the family; in common parlance this means, "You go your way and I'll go mine."

There can be no doubt but that marriage on this plane offers certain distinct advantages. Fully developed personalities, coöperating in the amenities and intimacies of the marital relationship, and pooling their personal and social resources, can create a satisfying type of family life, and there is ample evidence that many modern families are doing so successfully. Ask such persons what is wrong with the contemporary family, and they will answer: "Nothing. Positively nothing. We are having a finer and higher type of family life than people have ever had."

On the other hand, it must be obvious that there are definite dangers to marriages consummated on the foregoing bases. When one marries on the romantic plane, one tends to unmarry for the same reason. When one marries for personal happiness and fulfillment, then it follows that one must leave the mate for the same reason, i.e., when those ends are no longer served. If living with Jane Smith is essential to one's fullest personality development in 1949 as no one else can be, then by the same token, Mary Brown may be the indispensable one by 1952. If this be the basis of marriages, then obviously when the basis disappears, the marriage is over. To go your own way *within* the family may lead you right out of your own and into someone else's family.

We have emphasized thus far the role of student demands and interests in shaping the literature that has been produced in the field of marriage and the family. One other factor should be added, however; the predilections of the persons who have produced that literature. Zimmerman has called attention recently to this factor.

While there are many exceptions [he writes], it is a truism that family doctrine in Western society has been a product of unfamilistic persons. . . . This very characteristic may be partly responsible for the unrealism and extremism of family social theories in the West. Intellectual leaders in the West have held the most extreme views on the family, from complete worship of the family system to direct suggestion for its abnegation. Consequently, Western sociological theory of the family seems almost never to have attained and held for any great time a common sense of "rule and reason."[1]

Stated directly and specifically, this charge, made by a number of present-day critics, is that many of the leaders in the field of family study are persons who, for varying reasons, have not led normal family lives. Some of them, it is pointed out, are intellectuals, limited in their range of human contacts and experience; others are unmarried; many are childless; still others have been warped by personal domestic experiences; few of them have been family men and women, with normal and wholesome family experience. The extent to which this charge has been true historically has been checked by Zimmerman; the extent to which it is currently correct could be made the basis of an interesting future inquiry.

What has just been said must not be interpreted to mean that the entire literature on the family has been produced to meet the demands of romantic youth and modified by the predilections of unfamilistic persons who specialize in its study. This would be unfair to some highly competent social scientists who

[1] Carle C. Zimmerman, *Family and Civilization*, New York, Harper & Brothers, 1947, p. 674.

have made valuable contributions to our understanding of a highly complex field of human relationships. The conclusion seems inescapable, however, that much of our family literature has been the product of these factors, with the result that such problems as mate selection, how to know if it is love, courtship behavior, the honeymoon period, sex adjustment in marriage, the control of pregnancy, and personality patterns within the family have received a great deal of consideration, to the neglect of other aspects of family life. These obviously are the problems which grow out of an emphasis upon romance and individualism. Moreover, it must be admitted that they are of great importance, and that students of the family have developed considerable insight in these specialized areas.

Some Neglected Aspects of Family Study

It would be interesting, by the way of contrast, to speculate on what the literature of the family would be like if it had been developed primarily to meet the demands of middle-aged couples, married, let us say, more than fifteen years. Or if it had come into being for an audience of young married couples with children. Or if it had been developed inductively on the basis of scientific studies of family operation.

To mature students, with normal family experience, the relative neglect of two phases of family life has been particularly noticeable. One of these is the family's role in the continuity of life and of culture. The importance of this role is proved by the whole impressive length of human history. To understand this, it is necessary to go back to the fundamentals of human experience and ask: Why is the family? Why and how did it come to develop? What purpose does it serve? What is its function in the cosmic and eternal scheme of things? Briefly stated, the answer is this: The family is man's, nature's, and God's device for the perpetuation, not only of the race but also of civilization. The family is the connecting link between successive generations. It serves to reproduce mankind chronologically, i.e., biologically and culturally. Other functions of the family are secondary and incidental.

Full appreciation of this role of the family results in a whole new range of emphases and problems. These have to do with the responsibilities rather than the erotic satisfaction of married life; the main consideration now comes to be the continuity of family life and how it can best serve its basic functions. Interest shifts now to ways in which family life can be promoted, rather than upon the irreducible minima of enjoyment to be obtained from it. Each family sees itself as one version of the current generation; each generation is but a passing trustee of the life stream.

Not only does the family maintain the race biologically, but also culturally. It is this which distinguishes man from the other animals, and the human family from the mating pair at pre- human levels. What the other animals learn dies with them; what we learn we accumulate and transmit to the next genera- tion. It is this that we have in mind when we speak of the role of the family in cultural continuity.

Another phase of family study, relatively neglected, is that of its internal life. Of studies of the effect of social changes upon the family, there are plenty; that the family conditions and molds the personalities of its members, especially the younger members, has received a good deal of attention; how the family disintegrates in our modern culture has had perhaps undue emphasis; but how does the family operate? How does it work, and how does it do its work? What are the means it uses to accomplish its purposes? What are families like on the inside? What mechanisms make for smoothness in family operation? What factors make for family solidarity?

Our conviction of the importance of this approach to the family led us a number of years ago to seek to study and under- stand the mechanism and operation of families from the inside. Our analyses of family table talk, family modes of expression, the bilingual family, the role of guests, the significance of do- mestic servants,[3] the part played in family life by domestic

[3] James H. S. Bossard, *The Sociology of Child Development*, New York, Harper & Brothers, 1948, chapters VIII to XII, inclusive.

animals,[4] have been results of this effort. They have been presented as so many facets of family life from within.

Family stability, it seems important to emphasize, is an achievement in group living. In this process of living together, there are certain techniques which make for success; others which tend toward failure. It is our conviction that these techniques need to be identified, understood, and evaluated. Too much attention is paid to the rights and pleasures to which the individual is entitled by way of by-product to married group life; too little to the techniques by which they may be obtained. We have come to think that not only can these techniques be identified and studied, but also that they can be cultivated consciously.

rituals

The Concept of Ritual

In analyzing family life from within, our attention came to focus early in our studies upon certain forms of family behavior so recurrent as to suggest the term "habit," and yet having about them aspects of conscious rigidity and a sense of rightness and inevitability not generally associated with mere habits. They were habitual forms of family behavior, but with added features that made them more than habits. We came ultimately to think of these as family rituals. A more adequate definition of ritual in general and of family ritual in particular is attempted in the next chapter. We shall speak of ritual here as meaning a pattern of prescribed formal behavior, pertaining to some specific event, occasion, or situation, which tends to be repeated over and over again. As it develops, it tends to demand relatively punctilious observance, admitting of no, or at least very few, exceptions or deviations. As time goes on, it often becomes ceremonious, and sometimes solemn. Ritual is something to be done, not something to be thought out.

Ritual may arise about, and develop in respect to, any aspect of family life. In an earlier day, many families held devotional services in which the father was the leader but in which every-

---

[4] James H. S. Bossard, "The Mental Hygiene of Owning a Dog," *Mental Hygiene*, July, 1944, pp. 408-13.

one was expected to participate. This practice still continues, particularly in certain parts of this country, although its over-all prevalence has undoubtedly declined. Because of the older tendency to restrict the use of the term "ritual" to religious ceremonials, family rituals may be thought of by some contemporary readers as confined to such and similar practices and, since these have declined in frequency, may tend to think that the subject is of declining importance. As our study will show, this is far from the truth.

In many families the meal is highly ritualized, with a ceremony of carving and serving, of seating arrangements (such as no one sitting down until Mother is seated). Many of the rituals of family life have to do with etiquette; others, with the attitude of children toward parents. Or they develop as a part of the routine of child care. One who takes a child for a walk on Sunday afternoon, or reads the comic strips on Sunday morning, or reads a fairy tale before bedtime, and repeats the event several times, is very apt to discover that subsequent developments turn these practices into rituals. Again, many rituals center around holidays, such as Hallowe'en, Thanksgiving, Christmas, New Year's Day and the Fourth of July. In all these instances, a pattern of social behavior develops within the family, which each member of the group is expected to observe as a part of the group functioning.

Ritual obviously, then, comprises much of the behavior of which a family is proud and of which its members definitely approve. As a phase of family life, it is what the family sees about itself that it likes and wants formally to continue. Thus it seems essential for an understanding of family life that we study this: it may be highly important for the happiness of families that we seek to encourage and promote it. It may be that if mates agree on what they want thus consciously to promote in family life, and how to promote it, that we have identified an agency and area of family rapport. Possibly family tension and discord may be the inevitable price of differentials in ritualistic experiences and loyalties in the respective family backgrounds of the mates. Other studies of family failure and success have shown how significant such differences in background may be.[5] Ritual has been referred to as the core and essence of culture; we are inclined to think of family rituals as the hard core in a cultural approach to the study of the family. In fact, the longer our studies of the inside of family life have continued, the more we have come to wonder if ritual may not be the best one starting point for the study of family life, just as it has long been recognized as the best one for the study of religion. The first analytical comprehensions of religious phenomena were based on the observations of the ceremonies of believers. Further amplification of the points thus lightly touched upon here will be found in subsequent chapters.

At any rate, we are presenting herewith a pioneer study of ritual in family living. It is based on data gathered from more than four hundred families. Consideration of the theoretic bases, and of the details of this study, have occupied our attention over a number of years. This study is, so far as we know, the first systematic one of the subject. It is bound, therefore, to reveal many of the defects of a pioneering study. Obviously, it leaves unconsidered many problems arising in connection with family rituals, particularly in their relation to associated phenomena. Of many of these we are fully aware; and some of them, at least, we hope to deal with more adequately in future publications.

Introductory Forecast

A brief forecast of the succeeding chapters may serve to orient and, it is hoped, to intrigue the reader. Possibly, too, if one knows where one is going, there is increased alertness to the signs that point in that direction. The next chapter deals with the meaning of ritual. First there is a survey of definitions by leading scholars, showing how their conceptions of ritual have varied and changed through the years. Identifying the basic elements involved in their conceptions, a definition for purposes of the present volume is formulated with illustrative cases from

[5] Ernest W. Burgess and Leonard S. Cottrell, *Predicting Success and Failure in Marriage*, New York, Prentice-Hall, Inc., 1939.

the material included in our study. The changing nature of ritual is also shown as reflected in this material, which covers a period of about eighty years.

Then follows a chapter summarizing our study of family rituals as revealed by writers of autobiographies. This is our control group, so to speak, for all these writers presented their material on family ritual before the present study was conceived; in some cases, before the authors were born.

Alongside of the material from formal published autobiographies is presented, in the next chapter, another summary, self-revealed but unpublished and presented in less formal manner than the autobiographical material. These are accounts of family rituals as described by university students to whom the project was presented and whose coöperation in our study was enlisted.

Chapter 5 concerns itself with the trends in family rituals. What changes in the nature and various other aspects of rituals have occurred through the years? Our answer covers a period of two-thirds of a century, i.e., the years 1880-1946. This covers approximately two generations, and the period of rapid social change of modern times.

Recent scholarship in sociology has revealed another dimension for interpretive studies, as measured by the yardstick of class differentials. Chapter 6, therefore, breaks down the subject of family ritual on a class basis, and we present a study in which differentials in such rituals are revealed as found in upper, middle, and lower class families.

But ritual varies with the age and stage of development of the family, as well as with the class status. Utilizing the family cycle as a conceptual tool, Chapter 7 reveals significant changes from one stage of the cycle to another—changes in degree of success in establishing rituals, tensions in their maintenance, or extent of conformity to or derivation from them.

To emphasize further this development approach, the next chapter presents a three-generational study of family ritual. Stressed here are the processes of family ritual: innovation, continuity, and discontinuity.

Following this, there is the chapter on family ritual and family integration. This is a summary chapter, presenting the thesis of family as a relatively reliable index of family integration, family happiness, and family continuity.

Concluding the volume is a chapter dealing with the methodology involved in this particular study. The sources of the material utilized are described, together with our evaluation of them. Readers who are particularly interested in this phase of the work may wish to turn to this chapter early in the reading of the volume; others may be content to wait until the end for a brief explanation of how we have tried to get inside the family to see a part of its "ticking process."

2

Family Ritual: Its Meaning and Changing Nature

Something About Ritual in General

WORDS TEND to be known by the company they keep. Sometimes that company becomes a jealous mistress, taking a word and keeping it for its own particular use and purpose. Many a word expressing an idea of general importance comes to be taken over by some particular group and is henceforth thought of mainly or wholly in that connotation. The word "ritual" is a case in point.

"Ritual" is a very old word, but it has kept company throughout its history mainly with two groups of persons. One of these has consisted of students of religion. They have emphasized ritual a very great deal, although not always for the same reasons. Some have seen it as the origin of religion, others as a technique of magic and worship, and still others as a part of the ethical and control system of religion.

The other group has been anthropologists, and their studies of primitive people have featured the subject of ritual prominently. Many anthropologists have identified ritual as one of the obvious and inescapable characteristics of primitive culture, with forms that are highly visible, and that pervade every field of human activity. But they, too, have emphasized chiefly its role in the development of religion, so that references to ritual are everywhere interwoven with discussions of magic, myth, taboo, totemism and the like.

lengthened. Nothing ever deterred Kay and Jane from being at home on Christmas Eve; dates with boys, even after their engagements had been announced, were not made; once Kay did not accept an invitation to a much desired trip so that she might be at home for "the reading." After Kay's marriage, she and her husband came to her parents' home on Christmas Eve in order to be present for the event. This practice has been continued down to the present time, both by Kay and her husband and by Jane and her husband. Last year, the father read to both daughters, their husbands, three grandchildren and grandmother.

2. *The Hair-washing Ritual.* "Thursday night was always hair-washing night at our house. Religiously, when that night of the week rolled around, Mother would march me upstairs, and make sure I got into the tub before I had a chance to jump into bed. I usually knew when it was time for this ordeal by listening to the radio. It never failed that when Rudy Vallee would come on the air, Mother would call: 'Come on, sister, it's time for your hair washing.' To me this was worse than a dose of castor oil. 'But all little boys and girls have to have their heads washed,' Mother would say. 'Look at Daddy and me, we are grown people, and we have to wash our hair.' 'All right,' I would say, 'but my little girl won't ever have to wash her hair.' This would make Mother laugh, but all the same she would dump me into the tub and start scrubbing away. When the Rudy Vallee program went off the air I was delighted, for I knew the job was over and I would not have to go through such torture for another week. But now it is many years later, and other radio programs are on the air, but Thursday night is still hair-washing night in my life."

3. *The Saturday Night Egg-eating Ritual.* "I was in my last year in High School when the depression came. Our family was hard hit by it. I succeeded in getting a summer job to help out. The first Saturday I worked, Daddy and I came home at about the same time (ten o'clock) in the evening. I remember that I fried some eggs and made some coffee for us that night. While we ate, we talked about our experiences at work, then

we put our weekly wages on the table and, with Mother coming in, we planned our expenditures for the week ahead. Thus began a practice which has continued at our house ever since. Every Saturday night we meet in the kitchen of our home at ten o'clock. Eggs are fried, and coffee and cocoa are served. Then we talk about our work, the experiences of the past week, the family income, our plan for family expenditures, and other matters of family importance. Often these family sessions last until after one o'clock. Six years ago I was married, but my husband and I have kept our weekly date with Mother and Dad. None of us ever lets anything interfere with these Saturday night get-togethers. They surely have become a ritual in the life of our families."

4. *The Saturday Afternoon Gift Ritual.* "Saturday afternoon held a very special ritual in our family: the bringing home of the Reading Terminal [a well-known Philadelphia market] package. My father would leave his office at noon, go to the Terminal for his lunch, and then shop. Mother and Sister and I waited for him in the den, and he would come straight up and put a huge parcel on Mother's lap. The scissors were ready on the table beside her. There was always a pound of Wilbur buds for Mother: her favorite candy. There were always two one-half pound boxes of hard candies for Sister and me. The other contents varied from week to week, but usually included all sorts of exotic fruits, fresh, candied and preserved; nuts; dates; and cookies. We all sat still until each package had been opened and exclaimed about, sampled a bit of this and that, and then the party was over until next Saturday. At the end of the party, Daddy handed our allowances to my sister and me, and we rushed out as fast as we could to spend them."

These cases will serve at once to illustrate the nature of family rituals as conceived in this study, and also some of the difficulties involved in their more careful identification. Case 1 obviously is a ritual, long continued, with fully established rigidity and attendant family ceremonial. Case 2 is rather less clear cut and might be termed, with strict use of language, a family routine or habit. This distinction, which may interest

some of our readers, seems to us to be of less importance, for we came early in our inquiry to conclude that we were dealing with a process of family interaction, in which a series of stages could be determined. In the earlier stages, one found chiefly experiments in meeting some problem or interest of family relationships. If successful in achieving these ends, the particular procedures came to be repeated over and over again. Ultimately, rigidity and manifestations of conscious group approval, such as various ceremonial features, begin to appear, often with the establishment of elaborated family rites.

These facts also suggest certain broader implications of our study. Viewed in their broader implications, such cases are more than family rituals: they are snapshots, so to speak, of social origins. That is, one could assume legitimately that the origin of any custom followed the development of family rituals. Social development is a continuing process. Folkways, mores, customs, and ritual are always being born, and some survive for a history that looms ahead rather than trails behind.[2]

Characteristics of Contemporary Family Life and Rituals

This introductory exposition of family ritual would not be complete without reference to certain changes in the nature both of family life and of its accompanying rituals. It is this very fact of change which has led so many modern students to overlook the existence and importance of ritual in family living. While there is general realization of sweeping changes in modern times in the characteristics of family life, the fact that many of these changes should go hand in hand with similar changes in family rituals has not generally been appreciated. A brief summary of these trends at this point will help therefore in the further understanding of the nature and role of ritual in family living.

Keeping in mind the kinds of change in current family life

[2] We are indebted to both the late Raymond Kennedy, professor of sociology at Yale University, and Jessie Bernard, professor of sociology at Pennsylvania State College, for calling attention to this possibility in the use of our material.

identified by present-day sociologists, the case material on which this volume is based, including some four hundred family records and extending over almost a hundred years (1856-1949), seven trends may be clearly identified. These trends are: (1) from predominance of the religious to predominance of the secular; (2) from a large group to a small group; (3) from a stable to a mobile group; (4) from an adult-centered to a child-centered family; (5) from a communal family-ideology to a democratic one; (6) from an integrated to an individualized group; (7) from a neighborhood-enclosed family to one isolated in an urban environment. Brief comment on each of these trends will help to clarify their meaning in relation to family ritual.

1. *The trend from a religious-dominated to a secular-minded family.* This change in the family, noted by so many contemporary students, affects both the looks and power of its rituals. In a society where the religious, or supernatural, invades and controls every aspect of life, ritual, though it may spring from a completely secular need, soon comes under the control, and receives the power of the sacred. It also puts on the dress of the sacred. And so it becomes both religious and spectacular in nature. In a society where the religious and secular are autonomous, much intra-family ritual remains both secular and simple. As an example, Henke writes: "The rise of the scientific attitude in its various manifestations means the death of many old notions. In the case of disease, for instance, demon possession and its cure, exorcism, could no longer hold their own where a scientific treatment of disease was discovered. . . ."[3] This does not mean, however, that there are no longer any rituals surrounding illness. The ritual, thus changed, builds its "mustness" on a secular and intra-family basis and not on fear of the supernatural. Though people today seldom dress in a frightening costume and beat the air with sticks in order to drive out the evil spirits, families have very special procedures surrounding illness. Such procedures involve not only the uses of certain medicines and medical devices, but fre-

[3] Henke, *op. cit.*, p. 58.

quently require a special room, bed, games, food, and bathing techniques. Often each member of the family has a specific ritualistic role in relation to the ill member. These rituals, though they have lost in pomp and rigidity, are called forth by the same anxiety and desire to do something constructive that motivated the primitive. They exist, but they are changed.

2. *The trend from a large group to a small group.* In a large primary group, like the tribal or large kinship group family, many persons perform the same rituals. When the tribe gathers under the council tree, or even when all of the VanSants hire a public assembly hall once a year for a family conference, their ritual is of a public nature, and highly visible. In the Chinese family, where many generations lived together and handed down exact practices to each new generation, rituals of family life, including everything from the time to rise and what to wear to how to feed aged members, were codified, and can be read in complete fullness today.[4] But when Mary and John go to their mother's bedroom with a tray of lemonade and cookies every Saturday night before retiring to discuss family problems, who else knows that they do so, or that every detail surrounding that evening meeting has become as thoroughly ritualized as was the older council meeting? Spencer has made this comment on ritual:

A chief reason why little attention has been paid to phenomena of this class . . . is that while to most social functions there correspond structures too large to be overlooked, functions which make up ceremonial control have correlative structures so small as to seem of no significance. That the government of observances has its organization, just as the political and ecclesiastical government have, is a fact habitually passed over, because, while the last two organizations have developed, the first has dwindled: in those societies, at least, which have reached the stage at which social phenomena become subjects of specialization.[5]

When the structure is entirely confined to the intimacy of

[4] See, *The Li Ki, The Texts of Confucianism, I°X*, Part III, Oxford University Press, 1885, pp. 449-464, tr. by James Legge.

[5] Spencer Herbert, *Principles of Sociology*, New York, D. Appleton and Co., II, 227.

a modern family bedroom it is very easily overlooked. Exclusiveness and intimacy seem to be a mark of modern family ritual.

3. *The trend from a stable to a mobile group.* Mobility has a definite influence on family ritual. First of all, when an immediate family unit breaks away from the milieu of the grandparent generation, the pressure to preserve the traditional ritual is lessened. Then, many rituals depend upon a certain physical setting, or upon definite material objects for their function. Those rituals must change in a different setting. The ritual of going to Grandmother's every Sunday and of meeting all one's aunts and cousins, while Grandfather reads from the family Bible and makes any new entries in its records, obviously cannot survive intact when aunts and cousins and family Bible are half a continent away. This does not mean that the habit of the Sunday family gathering must die out, but its content must change.

4. *The trend from an adult-centered to a child-centered family.* Along with a radical change in the whole idea of the child's relative place in the family, one finds a tendency, first, toward more "child-centered" ritual, and, second, toward a change in the emphasis of the content of the family rituals which function as control or education, from one of narrowly channelizing behavior to one of liberating and guiding potentialities. There is, for instance, less of the ritualistic gathering of the youngsters around the feet of the family patriarch for a period of instruction, and more of the ceremony which entails joint enterprise and display of individual talent.

5. *The trend from a communal family-ideology to a democratic one.* Henke has written that rituals are instituted in two ways. "The first is through trial and error without even the crudest thought. The second is where voluntary attention becomes the organ for manipulating the outside world, or in other words, where thought enters in and helps in bringing about an adjustment."[6] (Henke does not mean here that ritual generated at the conscious level remains at that level. As it

[6] *Op. cit.,* pp. 39-40.

becomes crystallized, it becomes an habitual, unconsciously performed pattern of behavior, until attention again brings readjustments.) As revealed in case histories, the trend from the communal type to democratic type family seems to create ritual more frequently in the second manner and less in the first, and for two reasons. First, democracy teaches its followers to think for themselves, and it gives them the right to express their thoughts. It is probably true that in a democratic family any series of family acts which tend to become routinized through mere trial and error has less opportunity of remaining at the unconscious level and in rigid form than it would in a communal-trained family. The members of the democratic family will speak out and demand revisions to their individual tastes, and in this way their rituals come to be constructed at the conscious level, until they are sufficiently adjusted to individual needs and can then become, for a time, unconsciously habitual. This means that ritual in the contemporary family can often be a source of tension, at the point when it, as an habitual pattern, is rising to the consciousness of individual members as being no longer exactly fitting. It can also mean that greater flexibility in the adjusting of an habitual pattern by conscious thought can relax the tensions with comparative ease and prevent a sort of family cultural lag. The second reason is but the opposite face of the same democratic concept. A ritual here is not often imposed relentlessly, and in toto, upon the whole group. Freedom of choice remains to the individuals. Separate members may participate in the group rituals wholly, in part, or not at all, with considerable individuality.

6. *The trend from the integrated to the individualized family group.* It seems to be clearly indicated that the family, in changing from a group in which most activities were performed together, to one in which there are relatively few occasions for common participation, effects a parallel change in their ritual. The more narrowly restricted the general participation in family life, the more narrowly restricted rituals tend to be both in number and scope. This does not in all cases, however, suggest non-existence or a weakening of the remaining ritual.

To the contrary, in some families limited in time- and interest-sharing, some few rituals are clung to tenaciously and with fierce emotion, as the adhesive in family unity.

7. *The trend from the neighborhood-enclosed family to the urban isolated family.* Finally, as personal contact between separate families decreases, the most intimate ritual becomes much more personalized from family to family. Spontaneous genesis of ritual in the family circle seems to have the ascendancy over its adoption by assimilation or contagion. Though many homes practice the same sorts of rites, because they grow up around the common rhythm and needs of daily family living, the contents of these rites vary individually. They are originated as experiments in one small, separated group; and take hold as they prove to be the best ways for that one group. Success and the strength of habit may cause them to spread vertically from one generation to the next, but they are less apt to spread horizontally in exact form.

The Changing Nature and Extent of Family Ritual

The family rituals described in this volume cover a period of about eighty years. The number of cases, considered by successive decades, seems large enough to warrant some conclusions concerning the extent and nature of family rituals.

First, ritual remains, or has continued as, an integral part of family life during the period covered. In other words, ritual is not dying. Like other social phenomena that students have "buried" from time to time, it remains an active and healthy corpse. Rituals which have taken form within the past few years and center about some event of contemporary significance are described as intently and viewed as seriously as those which obtained in the eighteen-seventies.

Second, ritual in family living has become secularized in large measure. This tendency is clearly revealed, and its recognition is highly important. Once ritual is thought of as a process of interaction rather than in terms of some pietistic end, then sherry before dinner may become as much a ritual as family prayers before going to bed; and listening to a Sunday night radio program may be the center of a ritual complex as much as the reading of the Bible.

One of the strongest rituals in our family concerns the use of the radio. Ever since I can remember we have had a radio, and ever since I can remember we have listened to the same programs. The program, "One Man's Family," has been criticized for the last five years by my brother and me, but it still survives. Sunday evening started out at six o'clock with an 1847 Roger's Brother play and ended with the eleven o'clock news. The programs in between have never varied. The Lux Radio Theater at nine on Monday evenings will be a must for my mother and dad until they go deaf or an atom bomb falls on the studio. (Selected from source material.)

An increasing proportion of present-day rituals, then, have to do with the secular rather than with the religious, a fact which opens up the whole subject of ritual in the study of contemporary family life.

Third, the question of the changing extent of ritual in family living is a difficult one. The present study makes no effort to present quantitative evidence on this subject, and we record here simply certain impressions. Family ritual seems to us quite clearly to be on the increase, so far as the number of rituals observed is concerned. The reasons for this seem fairly clear. The modern family, and particularly the city family, has more leisure to devote to the refinements of family living, and ritual quite obviously involves the ceremonial use of leisure. Again, the enriched variety of contemporary life offers a greater number of things for families to do together, if they are so minded. Also, there is the pressure of mass advertising, which seeks to build up and exploit the commercial aspects of many rituals, such as gift giving, card sending, observance of holidays, and the like.

The foregoing conclusion is confined to the change in the number and variety of rituals observed. There is a related question which is entirely distinct: Is the overall ritualizing of the individual home increasing or not? Current rituals may be more numerous and more varied, but of shorter duration and of less overall significance. This question is a pertinent one: the data available to us do not permit more than a suspicion in the direction of a negative answer.

The question of the changing extent of ritual in family life is complicated by the effects of the changing size of the family. This poses the problem: Do family rituals vary with the size of the family? The material at our disposal makes an unequivocal answer difficult, if not impossible. Taken as a whole, our data suggest that the larger the family, the more numerous and rich the rituals, whether the family was large by number of children, or was made large by the inclusion of relatives and family servants. This conclusion was particularly buttressed by the material obtained from published autobiographies, which is dealt with in a subsequent chapter. On the other hand, if the material on large urban families at the lower income levels is considered separately, the number and variety of family rituals are relatively small. It would appear that, given education and economic ease, or at least comfort, the larger families had special opportunities for ritual development, and took full advantage of it. One even gets the impression that the desire for large families and love for a ritualized home life go hand in hand. A careful reading of a recent best seller[7] gives a similar impression. The small families in this study, by way of contrast, reported fewer rituals. Younger persons included in the study reporting a complete or relative lack of family rituals came mostly from small families, often one-child families. And yet here exceptions must be noted. In the material from one-child families, one discovers a good deal of the formalized, repressive kind of ritual that is deliberately dwelt upon as the hope of the family, as well as the prolonging of rituals of intimate family association, in order to keep the only child from getting away from the family fold. Also, a small immediate family, if in extended contact with a number of kinfolk, may develop considerable ritual. Finally, it is but necessary to recall in this connection facts previously men-

[7] Frank B. Gilbreth, Jr., and Ernestine Gilbreth Carey, *Cheaper by the Dozen*, New York, Thomas Y. Crowell Co., 1948.

tioned in this chapter, that the small family makes for narrowly restricted rituals, as well as for their personalized development. Rituals that are confined to the intimacies of a small group cannot match the color and impressiveness of those which the large group tends to develop, and thus are likely to be overlooked by the student as well as by the small family members themselves.

Summary

1. The subject of family ritual as a project for research in the modern family may have been neglected largely because of inadequate and confused conceptions of the true nature of ritual.

2. The term "ritual" is used in this study to mean a prescribed procedure, arising out of family interaction, involving a pattern of defined behavior, which is directed toward some specific end or purpose, and acquires rigidity and a sense of rightness as a result of its continuing history. Thus defined, many rituals can be identified as existing in present day families.

3. Because the modern family is so unlike the primitive family, its interactive processes accumulate a content quite dissimilar to that in the primitive family and with which we have become more familiar. However, the ritual of the modern family seems to have certain characteristics which grow directly from the nature of the group. Some of these characteristics, in comparison with familiar rituals, are that they tend to be: (a) more secular and simple; (b) more intimate and less public; (c) less traditional, i.e., of shorter duration in their original rigidity; (d) less repressively and autocratically prescribed; (e) more frequently of the consciously constructed and adjusted type; (f) more narrowly restricted in number and scope; and (g) more personalized to particular family groups.

4. Conclusions concerning the changing extent and nature of rituals in family living are: (a) ritual has been an integral part of family life during the eighty years covered by the present study; (b) ritual has become secularized in large measure; (c) the number and variety of family rituals seem to be

on the increase, but this does not mean that the overall ritual-izing of family life is on the increase; and (d) conclusions on the changing extent of family ritual are complicated by the effects of the changing size of the family. Since primitive rituals are considered to be symptomatic of the culture from which they derive, it is suggested here that current family rites, once identified and isolated, will also be symptoms of their respective group cultures. As such they may be profitable subjects for family study.

3

Family Ritual in Autobiographies

THE EXPLORATORY stage in our study of family ritual involved an examination of a hundred published autobiographies, to see to what extent the authors considered it pertinent to include references to family behavior patterns in their own experience which fell within the confines of our concept. Here were persons, presumably of some competence and prominence, who were not sociologists or professional students of the family, who were not prompted by any questionnaire or stimulated by interactive interviews to recall references to any particular features of family living. Would such persons write of what we have described as rituals?

A careful reading of these autobiographies easily led to the conclusion that a very significant part of family life has been almost wholly neglected by students of the modern family. For, although no thorough analysis of current family rituals has appeared, those autobiographers who earnestly tried to reproduce their early lives in book form described a large part of their family activities and behavior in terms of family rituals. It was, in fact, their organization of those regularly repeated procedures that framed the canvas revealing each family, and within which certain single events and crises came to have specific meaning in so far as they invaded the confines of a unique framework of usual acts and usual behavior. These rituals, arising out of some simple or random bits of family interaction, started to set, because they were successful or satisfying to members, and through repetition they "jelled" into very definite forms, expressing in terms of overt behavior how a particular family for a time was expected to react and did react under certain circumstances. Since these rituals, in some autobiographies, ruled over most of the normal, intimate aspects of day-to-day family life, they became very significant in describing both the nature of family interaction and some ways in which its culture was passed along to the children. If the life stories of these writers are at all representative of family life processes in general, they definitely suggest the value of giving current family ritual more careful consideration. As an exploratory beginning of such consideration, the autobiographers' family rituals are analyzed in this chapter.

The Source Material

The hundred published autobiographies examined for the material they contained on family ritual were chosen at random from those writers who included the period of their childhood. Seventy-three describe procedures which were unequivocally classifiable as family rituals, according to the definition used as the basis for this study. This ratio of 73 to 100, however, is misleading in one respect. Most of the autobiographies included material suggestive of some family ritual. However, none was so accepted for this study without this requirement: that the author actually illustrated the details of a prescribed procedure and one that was, for a certain period, a repetitive procedure. This means that many more rituals were apparent than are indicated numerically or are used as case material for this study.

Of the authors, fifty-two were men and twenty-one women.

The publication of their life histories extended from 1856 to 1946, and the percentages by years are as follows:

Years	Percentage of Total
1856-1900	8.6
1900-1909	5.3
1910-1919	5.3
1920-1929	14.3
1930-1939	45.2
1940-1946	21.3

More significant to this study is the fact that the case histories analyzed represented descriptions of childhood at home during a fairly well-defined era in modern family history. Over 80 per cent of the authors described rituals which were a part of family life during the years of 1880-1917. This is the period during which forces for secularization, mobility, urbanization, and individuation were gathering and showing their effects upon the family, but they had not yet reached the tornado-like velocity of the post World War I era. In the interests of examining rituals as products of their specific social setting, these rituals of 1880-1917 will be compared in a later study to a group of rituals described by present-day university students whose family life represents entirely the era after World War I and largely during the depression and World War II. However, this chapter attempts only to describe the family rituals of one specific era and to indicate some of their influences upon the families and individuals participating.

Kinds of Rituals Described

The occasions within the family life that stimulated ritualistic procedures were of very wide range, as was the variation in the numbers of authors who mentioned each kind. The types of ritual and the numbers of authors describing them were as follows:

1. Rituals surrounding formal schooling at home, or the preparation of home work—9

2. Rituals concerning lessons, or participation, in dancing or music—7

3. Reading rituals (for purposes other than formal secular or religious education—13 (Reading aloud was one part of many other kinds of family rites such as illness, bedtime, Sunday, etc.)

4. Summer vacation rituals—10

5. Rituals concerning allowances, money expenditures, and family pet economies—3

6. Sunday rituals—23

7. Religious rituals—17

8. Rituals for keeping time—2

9. Holiday and anniversary rituals—8

10. Rituals of retiring and arising—9

11. Mealtime rituals—11

12. Family recreation rituals—25

13. Bath and bathroom rituals—5

14. Rituals during illness—7

15. Rituals concerning family work activities—3

16. Disciplinary rituals—3

17. Family council—1

18. Homecoming rituals—4

19. Status-defining rituals—1 (Status definition was prominent in many rites. This one alone, though, was an example of a family rite of passage.)

20. Family moving-day ritual—1

Total—171

The remainder of this chapter is based upon an analysis of these rituals.

Attributes of Ritual

There is no attempt here to suggest ritualistic determinism. The hypothesis developed is that family ritual is an important conditioning factor, but only one factor. With this moderate point of view, and as a preface to subsequent evaluation of specific rituals, it is pertinent to examine certain attributes of all rituals indicated in the material which seem to give them special power.

1. First, they have the attribute of frequent, exact repetition. This means that even at the physiological level they carve deep-ridged pathways of reaction, and form patterns which are held to effortlessly and without much thought. They become integrated parts of family situation and individual personality because of their continuous directioning. This influence is seen in the materials studied when authors attempt to recall their early family life. They seem to recall most easily, and remember as the basic reality of their home life, those things which were habitual to it, even though they may think of them as one certain occasion. Frank Kendon, with considerable insight, realized this when he wrote: "I can recall the mixed warmth and cold of Christmas morning, when we children would wake before daylight to scramble out of bed for our filled stockings; but as soon as I begin to remember the actions and the conversations across the ghostly dark, I know I am not recalling an occasion, but a sketchy kind of knowledge of several occasions: not what we did then, but what we used to do."[1] Another aspect of the importance of repetition is that it is not only imposed but desired, and especially by small children. Arnold Gesell has noted that at about the age of two and one-half years a child has a very strong ritualistic sense of having everything at home in its usual place and done in its usual way. He may be very iron-willed about his demands and insist that each family member perform his ritualistic role precisely.[2] No doubt the rhythmic repetition of intimate family acts spells both confidence in right performance and predictability to a small individual whose experience is very limited and whose intellectual immaturity makes him unable to grasp universal permanences. Thus the reaction pathways are cut still deeper by insistence upon repetition.

2. A second attribute of the ritual is its social nature. It is not a performance in which one is alone. Henke has said: "The

[1] Frank Kendon, *The Small Years*, Cambridge University Press, 1930, pp. 39-40.

[2] Arnold Gesell, Frances L. Ilg, et al., *The Child From Five to Ten*, New York, Harper & Brothers, 1946, p. 347.

ceremony is always a social reaction . . . the various ceremonies are overt reactions out of a matrix which is nothing more or less than the social consciousness."[3] When this is translated into terms of family ritual, it means that they are acts which compel coördinated participation of people already emotionally inter-dependent. Many performances though related to family life are organized in an individualistic manner: rituals are not. There-fore, with special significance to children, a family rite is a dependable occasion of family social consciousness, when at least several members act with mutual recognition of their related roles. A feeling of belonging to a family and of not just living in it might well correlate with the frequency and intensity of these rites which are expressions of family social consciousness.

3. A third important attribute of the ritual is its emotional coloring, and this is closely related to its repetitious and social nature. From the repetition one comes to feel, without thought, that one's way of doing a thing is *the* way. When a different system calls one's own into consciousness, other emotions rise. Frank Kendon, again, has noted this in his own experience. Describing early visits to his grandparents' home, he writes:

I learned with surprise that all people do not eat milk and por-ridge in the same way. For granny taught me to dig a small pond, I called it, in the middle of my porridge, and to pour my cold milk into that. It was not the family way at home; there we let the milk fill the edges of the plate and mount, to some extent, the rounded plateau. But if granny's method was revolutionary, it was all the more exciting to try. . . . While I stayed with granny I did as granny did, and with new delight every morning; but I returned to family methods when I came home again, and did not change until, in due time, I was allowed to refuse porridge altogether. . . .

Their customs were then as different from ours as the customs of people in foreign countries are to-day. In our own family, father and mother sat side by side behind the tea-tray at the top of the table; in theirs, grandfather sat at one end and grandmother with her tea-urn at the other end of a very long table. It was with astonish-

[3] Frederick Goodrich Henke, *A Study in the Psychology of Ritualism*, University of Chicago Press, 1910, pp. 8-9.

ment that we saw how differently grandfather drank his tea or ate his cake; we, in our manners, lifted the cup from the saucer, and left the saucer on the table; but grandfather lifted both together, and while he drank held the saucer in his left hand under the cup in his right. In our system, too, there were two distinct stages of food at tea—the prose or bread-and-butter stage, and the poetical or cake, bun and biscuit stage. We children ate our bread-and-butter dutifully so that we might eat our cake with delight. But grandfather would make a barbarous sandwich of a slice of cake between two slices of bread-and-butter, and eating this, would thus enjoy both kinds of provender at one bite.[4]

The emotional attitudes called forth by this sudden recognition of differences may be attitudes of antagonism or protectiveness toward one's own ways. Each has its significance, and each was found in the life histories. But either reaction seemed to be linked with the specific family-social setting of the ritual. A rite, in its repetition, became not just a kind of behavior to the participators, but incorporated into itself all the sounds, sights, temperatures, touch sensations, and human relationships that always surrounded it. The combination produced a whole situation which was pleasing or unpleasant, and deeply so since it related to family social-consciousness. Augustus Hare describes his reaction, on this basis, to one ritual:

Of all the miserable days in the year, Christmas was the worst. I regarded it with loathing unutterable. The presents of the quintessence of rubbish which I had to receive from my aunts with outward grace and gratitude. The finding all my usual avocations and interests cleared away. The having to sit for hours and hours pretending to be deeply interested in the six huge volumes of Foxe's "Book of Martyrs," one of which was always doled out for my mental sustenance. The being compelled—usually with agonizing chilblains —to walk twice to church, eight miles through the snow or piercing marsh winds, and sit for hours in mute anguish of congelation, with one of Uncle Julius's interminable sermons in the afternoon. . . . Then, far the worst of all, the Rectory and its sneerings and snubbings in the evening. My mother took little or no notice of all this— her thoughts, her heart, were far away. To her Christmas was simply

4 Kendon, *op. cit.*, pp. 32 and 100.

"the festival of the birth of Christ." Her whole spiritual being was absorbed in it: earth did not signify: she did not and could not understand why it was not always the same with her little boy.[5]

Ray Stannard Baker presents a different reaction:

Sunday morning "prayers" were an institution in our Presbyterian household. I can hear my father talking with God; I can somehow *see,* as though I now stood aside with no real right to possession, I can see the little boy who was myself kneeling there on the carpet with his nose buried in the queer musty-smelling upholstery of the living-room chair, listening intently to what Father said to God. All the things I remember!—my father's broad back as he also knelt by his chair, his stiff white hair, his great beetling eyebrows with the eyelids under them trembling and sometimes partly opening, as seen by the little boy through the cracks between his fingers; the thin ankles and worn shoes of Aunt Amanda, and my mother's beautiful head with her delicate fingers thrust up into her soft hair, and the row of other little boys who were my brothers, kneeling more or less restlessly, each by his chair. I can see the house-plants in the warm window and our old cat curled in the Sunday morning sunshine on the sill just outside, and the rows of battered books in the cases, and the picture of Beatrice Cenci, beautiful but sad, in its golden frame, just above the stove. It was wrong, of course, to look through one's fingers when Father was talking with God, but I had already learned that one often did what he disapproved because it was so interesting or so delightful.[6]

A ritual setting such as this is apt to call forth fierce protectiveness, for deviation from any of its principles might threaten the whole structure that creates such deep physical and psychological well-being.[7]

[5] Augustus Hare, *The Story of My Life,* New York, Dodd, Mead & Company, 1896, pp. 190-91.

[6] Ray Stannard Baker, *Native American,* New York, Charles Scribner's Sons, 1941, pp. 31-32.

[7] For an excellent example, in literature, of the result of disillusion with an emotionally revered family ritual, see Joe Sinclair, *Wasteland,* New York, Harper & Brothers, 1946. In this novel, a Jewish boy whose most satisfying family experience had been the celebration of the Passover, cut himself off from it when he saw his family's lack of sympathy for it. Years later it took a skilful psychiatrist to show him that this crisis had separated him from Jewry, his family, and his own individual heritage.

Repetition, a social nature, and emotional coloring, then, are three attributes of ritual which, no matter what the specific content, impress rituals deeply upon groups and individuals participating in them.

Family Ritual as an Instrument in Culture Transmission

At the present time, it is believed that one of the most important remaining functions of the family is the transmission of the culture to successive generations. In a civilization as complex as ours this function must be highly selective in its performance. It has become, then, most important to discover exactly how culture is transmitted in the family and upon what bases selectivity rests. Ralph Linton has classified the content of culture into three categories: Universals, Specialties, and Alternatives. This last class of culture content has especial significance in its transference in the modern family. For, though Universals are common to all "sane, adult members of one culture group,"

there are in every culture a considerable number of traits (Alternatives) which are shared by certain individuals but which are not common to all members of the society . . . the elements . . . varying from the special and quite atypical ideas and habits of a particular family to such things as different schools of painting or sculpture. Aside from the nature of the participation in them, all these Alternatives have this in common: they represent different reactions to the same situations or different techniques for achieving the same ends. The cultures of small societies living under primitive conditions usually include only a moderate number of such Alternatives, while in such a culture as our own they are very plentiful. . . . Certain elements are transmitted in family lines. The members of one family may be taught to say a particular form of grace at meals . . . while other families transmit a grace of a different sort. . . . Most of the descriptions of cultures which are now extant are heavily weighted on the side of Universals and Specialties. This is due partly to the difficulty of obtaining information about the Alternatives, partly to a quite natural desire to make the description as coherent as possible. The only Alternatives which will be noted will usually be those which have large numbers of adherents. As a result, the participation of the average individual in the culture of his society is made to appear much more complete than it actually is, and the differences between different groups of individuals are minimized. Any one who has come to know a "primitive society" well can testify that its members do not show the dead level of cultural conformity which these reports suggest.[8]

If this be true, how much more misleading are reports of contemporary civilized groups if the Alternatives which are so much more numerous here are not thoroughly considered. Family rituals, as found in autobiographies, seem to be a fruitful field for investigating some of these Alternatives as they are selected and passed on to children. Four different aspects of such transmission are discussed in the following paragraphs: (1) A ritual was a family's specific conclusion, from its own experience, of the best way to meet a certain situation. Thus there was passed on to children, through ritual, a selected way of doing a thing—an overt behavior pattern. (2) The behavior pattern of a ritual was an expression of certain attitudes, largely parental attitudes. The behavior, then, became a concrete means of attitude communication between parents and children. (3) A ritual was a behavior pattern with a *purpose*. The whole ritual scheme of a family, therefore, objectified into behavior, and was one means of transmitting the family direction, or goals. (4) The material content of rituals, family-selected, became cultural tools for social participation of the children who inherited them. Though these four aspects are not wholly disparate, they will be treated separately here and, at the sacrifice of "the quite natural desire to make the description as coherent as possible," as many differences as material and space permit will be presented.

1. The autobiographers clearly showed rituals as selective transmitters of behavior patterns on the basis of race, creed, social class, economic status, educational level, urban or rural life, and other individual differences. Traditional Jewish rituals in the home, for instance, were mentioned by three authors. In one home they were preserved faithfully and passed down

[8] Ralph Linton, *The Study of Man*, New York, D. Appleton-Century Company, 1936, pp. 273-79.

as an honorable heritage. In a second home, they were abandoned for the family, but taught to the children so that they
might observe certain forms in the presence of respected orthodox Jewish guests. The third author was deprived of all knowledge of such ritual at home, and was repelled by it in his
grandparents' home, since it was so different from his family's
adopted Anglo-Saxon rites. Walter Damrosch and his wife
preserved the old-country traditional Christmas ritual with a
determination to pass it on intact to their children. Many of
the different forms surrounding Christmas rites varied according to traditional ethnic practices. The opening of gifts on
Christmas Eve, as one example, was a procedure in many
families of German descent, while Christmas-morning present-
opening was more characteristic of English-descended families.
Lest this seem insignificant, the reader may undeceive himself by discussing this difference with acquaintances. If he is
one who does the opening on Christmas Eve, he may be surprised at the ferocity with which he is accused of "cheating"
by a confirmed Christmas-morning opener. The whole family
behavior on Sunday differed markedly on the basis of the sect,
or individual family creed. Other, more intimate, rituals transmitted as obligatory patterns of life maintain:

that small children do not eat at table with parents; that they are
not only present at table but help with serving; that the whole family
is waited upon by servants; that the servant sits at table with the
family except when company comes; that meals are strictly utili-
tarian until Sunday guests make dinner an elaborate and proper social occasion; that children participate in guest situations only as
silent, well-behaved onlookers; that children always entertain guests
by showing off their talents.[9]

Ritualistic behavior passed on to children the practices:

that money is earned by the father, owned by him, and doled out
at his pleasure to wife and children, who have no real rights as con-

[9] For a discussion of the role of the family dinner table in culture transmission, see James H. S. Bossard, *The Sociology of Child Development*,
New York, Harper & Brothers, 1948, chapter VIII.

cerns family income; that it is earned by father who hands it over to mother to keep the household running; that money is to be enjoyed and spent freely by the whole family when it is obtainable, and is unimportant when it is scarce; that the whole family participates in paying financial obligations to others first, and then lives carefully on what is left; that one never makes a purchase without first comparing all advertisements to buy at the lowest price; that one buys only during bargain sales.

Through rituals, authors came to know:

that the bathroom is a place where one considerately takes turns, and calls out frankly in cases of emergency; that it is a place into which one sneaks surreptitiously and from which it is a profound shame to be seen emerging.

Rituals defined that:

family recreation means games, reading aloud, plays or concerts at home; or necessitates "going out": visits to friends, theatres, circuses or musicals.

They set as the one right pattern of life for some children:

that a family must go away from home for a summer vacation each year; that Saturdays are "fun" days; that certain holidays are celebrated and others ignored; that one takes a bath and changes underclothes at certain set intervals, daily, weekly; that one has a "best" suit of clothing reserved for special occasions; that one "dresses" for dinner each night; that a particular hour of the day is proper for rising, eating, retiring.

This is by no means an exhaustive list of the elements of obligatory family behavior passed on to the autobiographers through ritual, or of the differences from family to family. But these few examples may be sufficient to imply the importance of ritual in such a process.

2. Every ritual found in the case material conveyed to the reader some transferable parental attitude. The variety cannot

even be intimated here. But a few of the most common were these:

(a) Writers commented on their own attitudes toward illness in terms of the procedures which surrounded such occasions in their homes. Frazier Hunt writes:

It was always a joy to be just a little sick when Auntie [who was "Mother" to him] was around to take care of you. Not that I particularly liked to soak my feet in a mustard bath or to have my throat rubbed with goose grease and wrapped in a red flannel rag, but I did like the outpouring of affection and concern. Toward evening Auntie'd come into the bedroom with a pan of warm water, a washcloth, and a towel, and ever so gently she'd bathe my face and hands and comb my hair. Then she'd disappear and in a few minutes return with a tray and a white napkin over it, and there'd be a poached egg, milk toast, and a cup of sassafras tea.[10]

Corra Harris concludes a description of her family's rites during illness by saying: "I always felt blessed and happy at such times."[11] In contrast to these cheerful and philosophical attitudes toward indisposition, Hugh Faussett describes his father's "morbid" ritual. Hugh's mother had died, and the child himself was of weak constitution. His father:

. . . could indulge his anxiety only by insisting that I should be swaddled in flannel, should be surfeited with milk, and never be exposed without a thick coat to the dangers of a cold wind. This fear of the elements was to become more and more pronounced . . . until he shrank from every draught as the sure precursor of a chill and refused, even in mild weather, to have any windows open in the room in which he sat. With characteristic thoroughness he would have rooms "aired" at regular intervals when no one was occupying them, and then once again seal them against the cold currents which he feared.[12]

(b) Living as they did at a time when much of early formal education was received at home, nine autobiographers de-

[10] Frazier Hunt, *One American*, New York, Simon and Schuster, Inc., 1938, p. 17.
[11] Corra Harris, *My Book and Heart*, Houghton Mifflin Co., 1924, pp. 7-8.
[12] Hugh I'Anson Faussett, *A Modern Prelude*, London, Jonathan Cape, 1936, pp. 35-36.

scribed rituals surrounding it. Two authors whose parents made them learn their lessons while standing, and who stood beside them while they studied, mentioned their great awe of "learning," but felt oppressed by the responsibility. Others considered the education process as a grand and challenging game. These people were accustomed, when children, to having a whole large family gather around a table together each evening for a certain period, and engage in a kind of family-learning competition.

(c) Discipline, through regularity of practices, became a reasonable, constructive technique, such as a lecture from Father to explain the costs of vice; an amusing distraction from sin, such as the forcing of battling brothers to laugh together and so forget wrath; and a vengeful device, such as the hanging up of children by a roller towel, leaving them uncomfortable and helpless, with feet dangling.

(d) Through Sunday observances and family religious rites, the religion they symbolized came to be regarded as humane, valuable, and otherworldly; and also as fearful, repressive, and inescapable.

(e) Interesting examples of the communication of contrasting attitudes toward nudity and intimate functions of the body appeared in the rituals. The Milnes, at one time, had a bathroom with two tubs in it, and the rite was for Ken and Alan to "toss" for the larger tub, then play a game of "catch" with the soap, while keeping a sponge in place between the tub and the backs of their necks. A second author, however, describes his daily visits to the bathroom as a fearsome and secret rite between him and his nurse alone. So obligatory were the selected personnel and the furtiveness that when once another servant offered to substitute, the boy resisted to the point of humiliating accident.

(f) Even attitudes toward how one should greet a new day —eagerly, cheerfully, energetically; or morosely and reluctantly with as much procrastinating as possible—were communicated to the autobiographers by the habitual ways in which their parents awakened them, and the procedures surrounding their daily rising.

Small though this sample of attitudes be, even this list is significant in terms of individual differences. A psychiatrist could perhaps draw a fairly lifelike sketch solely on the basis of how a man feels about health, education, discipline, religion, the body and its functions, and how he behaves when he gets up in the morning.

3. One of the analytic steps in this study was to take the entire ritual structure of each family out of its context, strip it of any qualitative or attitudinal comments from the author, and let it stand alone as an individual-family framework of customary behavior in many recurring situations. This step proved to be very rewarding in that these stark frameworks let in light upon the directioning of family life with undoubtedly more clarity and veracity than the writers (beset by incomplete memory, inhibitions, and exhibitionism) could attain were they asked specifically to describe their family's goals and purposes.[13] As an example, a comparison of two of these excerpts will have to suffice. These two were selected on the basis of differences in ritual structure. But it is of interest to note that both families were religious, well-to-do, and well educated.

(a) The Carter family[14] enjoyed these rituals:

(1) daily—a cold bath; a breakfast for which every member of the family *had* to be on time; grace before the meal; family prayers after breakfast with the servants present and a very set routine; every-evening family gatherings with Father or Mother telling stories

[13] The authors suggest that students collecting personal-history documents by the method of presenting topical outlines to the subjects would find it profitable to include the topic of family rituals whenever part of their research is family goals, values, ambitions, etc. For here some of them will show up in terms of customary behavior and may be a helpful and enlightening supplement to what the subject *thinks* are his family goals, etc.

[14] John Franklin Carter, *The Rectory Family*, New York, Coward-McCann, Inc., 1937.

or reading aloud, a musical program by the children or games played with the whole family; bedtime for the children at nine o'clock, with individual and simple prayers before bed.

(2) Sunday—church; family prayers postponed till evening; a day of not doing things they did on weekdays; a chafing-dish supper, often with friends, prepared by Mother since servants were dismissed early; family prayers without the servants.

(3) holidays—"gave up" something for lent; "gorged" on Thanksgiving; had tree, presents, filled stockings, and carols on Christmas; fireworks on Fourth of July, which was a day restricted to family alone, on other holidays guests were invited.

(4) vacation—visit away from home inevitable for at least a month each summer, though their home town was a summer resort.

(5) medical—phosphate which it was a deadly sin not to drink before it stopped fizzing; castor oil with orange juice; "the basin"; "the croup kettle"; one trip to Boston to the hospital to see each new baby in the family; trips to Boston at regular intervals to visit dentist.

(6) discipline—recitation by quarreling brothers of a Bible verse which always made them laugh and make up; mouthwashing with soap; a lecture in Father's study; confinement for meditation and memorization of hymns.

(7) play—children teased Mother by calling her "Allie"; Mother teased Father by tickling; Father drove children out of his and Mother's bedroom at night by starting to take off his trousers.

(b) In contrast to the Carter family, the Hare family had these rituals:[15]

(1) daily—breakfast at 8 with Mother in dining room with doors open on to garden terrace; lessons with Mother or other relative after breakfast, a time of screaming, crying, and hearty bangs over the knuckles; at 12 a walk with Mother which was always in the nature of a lesson in botany, or a walk to a girls' school where Mother sat in the courtyard overhung with laburnums and taught the children; at 1, dinner, always roast mutton and rice pudding until, before the child was 6, the practice was instituted of elaborating on the delicious puddings to follow, only to have them snatched away just as the child was prepared to eat his, and he was then told to take them to some poor person in the village; after lunch the child read aloud, Josephus and Froissart's *Chronicles;* at 3 a drive in the carriage with Mother to visit distant cottages, often ending at the Rectory; at 5

[15] Hare, *op. cit.*

a half hour for the child to "amuse himself," during which he usually "heard the cat's lessons"; at 5:30 tea with his nurse in the servants' hall; evenings, Mother read aloud to old parents, at which time, if books were beyond child's comprehension, he was permitted to play with some ivory fish.

(2) religious—fasting on Wednesdays and Fridays, on which day there was no butter or pudding.

(3) holiday—Christmas: inappropriate presents from family with necessary show of gratitude from child; usual pastimes cleared away; required to sit for hours reading Foxe's *Book of Martyrs;* two 8-mile walks to church; evening visit to the Rectory.

(4) allowance—no regular time or amount set, but a periodic rapid calculation by Mother as to what child needed and an allotment of just that much and no more.

These total ritual structures in their comparison speak amply for themselves of the ways in which family selective culture of the most subjective sort can insinuate itself into the lives of children through rituals. Seen also in the ritual structures of families studied were, among others, these prime motives: the guiding of a talented member into a chosen career, social climbing; social respectability; worldly sophistication; and scrupulous unconventionality.

4. The material content of family rites varied 100 per cent in the autobiographers' case histories. But certain generalized similarities and differences were discernible, from family to family, in the tools which these rites offered to children.

(a) In the case of the many rituals which involved reading aloud, some families used only religious books; others only the classics, or histories; some, light novels of an admittedly "trashy" kind. Several families read all types of literature and also current newspapers and periodicals. In the case of an isolated farm family, reading was strictly of the last-mentioned kind, as being the family's only contact with the living outside world. Some authors mentioned no reading rites at all. Some wrote their own family literature.

(b) Music formed a large part of the content of rituals. For some families music meant family concerts; to others it was a program at a concert hall; and to still others, snatches of

songs upon rising and retiring. Families specialized in learning one instrument, or in having each member play a different
one. The kinds of composition made familiar through ritual
varied from the ponderous classics and opera, through senti-
mental melodies and folk songs, to collections of bawdy sea
ballads.

(c) Family games offered to children a significantly selected
list of accomplishments. There were, for instance, in different
families a noticeable emphasis upon: "gentlemen's" sports;
Bible bees; card games; the displaying of individual artistic
talents. Several families tended strictly to out-of-door games
of a simple nature, the walk being the thing. One family played
a game of languages; they spoke Roumanian one day, German
the next, and Greek the third day. A few families played dinner-
table question-and-answer games with rewards for correctness;
one restricting questions to the subject of opera; the others including a wide range of cultural subjects and current events.

(d) The actual roles which children took in rituals became
tools for useful action. For many children—and most of these
were farm-living and/or from modest-income families—these
consisted of knowing how to work, in the house or on the
farm. In a second group of families, the children learned how
to conform and how to study. These were usually small but
ambitious families. And in a third group, children learned
how to express themselves individually, while at the same time
participating socially. Children given these tools were ordinarily from larger families, but with comfortable incomes and
social standing.

(e) Finally, the range of social tools found in the ritual of
any one family must be considered. For comparison's sake, two
extremes are presented. Gertrude Lawrence, the incomparable
actress, described four childhood rituals: two were concerned
with how to be respectable, though devastatingly poor; and
the other two were leisure-time rituals which featured the
child as an infant phenomenon of an actress. To read her later
life, surprisingly enough, is to read almost exactly what one
might guess as a snap judgment solely on the basis of her hav-

ing early acquired such tools.[16] As a contrast, John Carter, whose whole family ritual structure was briefed a few pages earlier, writes this:

If anything, our home was too happy and too comfortable. Its outlook was frankly romantic—or perhaps truly realistic—for it really preferred good food, comfortable beds, good literature, good conversation and good music to the demands of the dusty world. . . . It was hard to leave such a sanctuary for the $30-a-week jobs and the hall bedrooms of city boarding houses, and the bitter struggle for riches and existence in the 1920's. We were, if anything, the heirs of an imperial tradition and were admirably equipped to serve as government officials or colonial administrators or something Kiplingesque and comfortably self-sacrificing, rather than to go out in a competitive industrial society to earn a living.[17]

Family Ritual and Family Interaction

These rituals of autobiographers were not just family-engineered canals through which culture flowed from one generation to the next; they were also dynamic processes of family interaction, and as such affected the groups themselves. The kinds of marks made varied with the kinds of rituals instituted. For brevity's sake, sharply contrasting illustrations will be selected to suggest the possibilities of family ritual as concerns family interaction.

1. Some rituals stimulated healthy family interaction. The mere formalizing of a time and a place for certain family members to be together for a purpose gave rise to increased family interplay and, in turn, to the enrichment of their rites. Enforced indoor confinement on Sundays resulted in regular reading aloud, family spelling bees, and question-and-answer games with rewards for the quickest. Pre-bedtime quiet periods around the dining-room table led to family magazines being written, concerts and plays organized, and displays of individual talents for the pleasure of all. One mother, with purposeful intent, insisted that her children report home from

[16] Gertrude Lawrence, *A Star Danced*, New York, Doubleday, Doran and Company, Inc., 1945.

[17] Carter, *op. cit.*, pp. 5-6.

school before going away again. Each day she prepared a snack for them when they reported. This resulted in their always being lured to their playroom attic, and remaining at home together. The study arranged for the children of one family as an inviolable realm of their own led to a children's club being formed which, in its description, sounds like a blessing upon family interaction.

The set of rules drawn up was to be as binding as the Decalogue. Like the Decalogue they were ten in number and chiefly negative. "Thou shalt not" was the tone, but they did not interfere with the liberty of the decently behaved.

Although Mother had nothing whatever to do with the affair, she must have been very glad of these rules, for they enabled the household to run smoothly without her having to harry, scold, or punish. Thus, in addition to regulations about work in the study, they forbade being late to breakfast (i.e., coming down after grace was said), going upstairs with boots on, omitting to brush your teeth, not hanging up coat and cap, and suchlike tiresome points for Mother to watch.

You may wonder how the club managed to enforce its rules. . . . Tom's plan was that we should be fined a penny, twopence, etc., up to a sixpence, according to a definite scale of charges every time we broke a rule. He bought an account-book, assigned a page to each of us, and reckoned up how much each owed at the end of the week.

Still you may wonder how the payment of the fines was enforced. It was quite simple—no payment, no entry to the study. Since the study was the heart of our home, to be shut out of it was misery. . . .

Tom soon found what he had no doubt hoped—that we had quite a nice little sum of money. He then unfolded his larger plan: the club was to be a real library. The shelves that had been decorated with childish fancies were cleared and made ready for books, and the first outlay was to be an additional bookcase that Charles had seen in Upper Street second hand. . . .

Imagine our excitement when we found that soon after the bookcase had been bought we had enough money to buy a *new* book. The number of books suggested, the meetings we held, the time spent in discussing the various possibilities—it all seems beyond belief today, when books are so cheap. . . . Surely no book was ever read and re-read and talked over as that first new volume, although we went on to buy many more. . . .

The outcome of our Library idea was an increased pride in the room itself. We took it in turn week by week to dust and tidy the study before breakfast. Since Tom didn't go to school he had time after breakfast to make a tour of inspection, and if he found any part undusted, or a book lying about, he charged the weekly cleaner any fine he thought right, "not exceeding sixpence." We never disputed his authority, for he took his own turn quite fairly and paid up his own fines. However, he had the privilege of being allowed to pay one of us to do his cleaning.

For small misdemeanours, such as doing sums aloud, shaking the table, or spilling ink, Tom executed summary justice by means of a big, round, black ruler, that always lay on the table like the mace in Parliament. "Hold out your hand," he would say very quietly, and down would come the blow, fairly softly if you were quick in holding out your hand. . . .

After a while we were in sufficient funds to take in some magazines. *Sunshine* and *Little Folks* for the younger ones, and *Cassell's Family Magazine* for us all. . . . *Cassell's Magazine* provided stronger meat, far more substantial than we get in the average magazine to-day. It had to last us a month, and I think every word of it found some reader in the family. When we had all read the portion of the serial story, and very definitely not before, we discussed endlessly at tea-time how the characters would turn out and who would marry whom.[18]

Such were the stimulating effects of their rituals upon family interaction in some autobiographers' homes.

2. Another type of ritual created antagonism or estrangement between family members. In all cases, this occurred when a ritual was imposed relentlessly by adults upon unwilling children. For example: a father who endlessly perpetuated his dead wife's memory by keeping all the rooms and all her belongings just as she had left them, guarding them against sun and wear, evoked from his son the remark that his father had denied his children the freedom essential to healthy growth.[19] A. A. Milne describes an infallible family rite of passage which caused tension: the hair cutting. All three boys had to wear Lord Fauntleroy hairdos until each one was "too big," and then the

[18] M. Vivian Hughes, *A London Child of the Seventies,* London, Oxford University Press, 1934, pp. 155-60.

[19] Fausset, *op. cit.,* pp. 29-36.

cutting ceremony took place. Alan and Ken were the two youngest, and after their older brother had acquired tonsorial manhood they clung together in their shame, but at least had comforting companionship. Then, Ken became "too big" sixteen months ahead of Alan. The author comments:

With the loss of Ken's hair something had gone out of our lives: our love of adventure, our habit of getting up early, even our desire to be alone together. . . . If I were a psychoanalytic critic, and if I thought that this Edwardian writer Milne were worth one of my portentous volumes, I should ascribe everything which he had done and failed to do, his personality as revealed in his books and hidden in himself, to the consciousness implanted in him as a child that he was battling against the wrong make-up.[20]

Finally, Norah James, ever an individualist, tells of how she escaped the threatened imposed ritual of "coming out" by insisting that if she were presented at Court she would make a scene in the throne room and disgrace the family.[21]

3. The relative position of family members was crystallized in many family rituals; for status, roles, and dominance relationships were clearly and repeatedly defined. One such rite was the nightly putting to bed of the current baby:

The procession started in the kitchen, the baby having been undressed, dried and swathed in night clothes and blankets by the kitchen stove. My mother bore her youngest. She was preceded by my oldest sister who, as attendant acolyte, and by reason of her age entrusted before the others of us, carried a lamp, lighted in winter, in summer ready for lighting. I followed my mother with a large pan, which contained the baby's bottles, his milk, and a small tin cup for heating the same over the lamp in question. My sister, two years my junior, grasped in one hand a creosote burner and in the other a tiny bottle of creosote against the croup, which might make its insidious appearance without the slightest warning. My brother brought up the rear of the line with an armful of extra blankets and diapers. We stopped for a moment in the library for my father to

[20] A. A. Milne, *Autobiography*, New York, E. P. Dutton & Company, Inc., 1939, pp. 84 and 27.

[21] Norah James, *I Lived in a Democracy*, New York, Longmans, Green and Company, 1939, pp. 47-48.

family rising that she always woke and jumped out of bed at that moment without an alarm clock or a call. Another can "sense" five o'clock because at that time the whole family always arrived home for the washing-up before dinner. To be clock-conscious, or un-clock-conscious, comes to be an indelible personality mark in adult life in our society, and one that matters. It would seem that such consciousness might be more deeply patterned by constant ritual habits than by repeated warnings and cursory penalties given in an unformalized atmosphere .

(d) *Rituals stressing individual rights in group life.* One of the most important phases of socialization is the learning of one's many statuses in relation to others under all sorts of circumstances, and the ability to adapt oneself to them. Rituals seemed to be particularly useful in this respect, for they emphasize status-relationships; and, even more important, the statuses changed from one rite to another. Quick adaptability to changes in dominance was practiced for the sake of group peace in family rites such as this. On evenings at home, whoever turned on the radio was the controller. But once he left the room, or stopped listening, any other member could then tune in another program and remain in control until his attention was diverted. This rite, a student felt, prevented many irritations over who actually was radio-master, because the rules for this status and its changes were carefully defined. Groups of family rituals showed the varying statuses of each member upon different occasions. Father was "served" and given the lounge chair because he earned the money and was head of the home; children did the dishes because Mother worked hard and was tired; Brother had to bring in the wood and dispose of the garbage because Sister was a girl; when guests were present, the children took over their parents' household chores because the parents were hosts; Mother and Father had a special evening out together because they were married. On a birthday, the lucky member ruled the household. During the Passover the youngest son had high honor in "asking the questions." At Christmas, children could "get away with murder." Certain family rites of passage emphasized vertical status changes. Such a one was described by a Jewish student:

A ritual which my family practices is the Bar Mitzvah, signifying the passing from childhood into manhood when each male member of the family reaches the age of thirteen. Before the Saturday morning gathering in the synagogue, the young boy must read certain Hebrew scripts from the Old Testament, deliver a speech of thankfulness to his parents for their devoted care throughout the years, and receive a final blessing of future success from the Rabbi before retiring from the pulpit. The occasion is celebrated with a party and the giving of gifts to the new "man."

Some less spectacular equivalents in Christian homes were: the presentation of a door key and driver's license as each child reached sixteen; the serving of tea or coffee at dinner after the fifteenth birthday.

As a contrast to the above rites, there may be cited one case in which the father was denied a dominant or prominent status in all family rituals. Control was maternal, and sometimes delegated to older girls. This, of course, was merely an expression of deeper cause, but through ritual it became overt, consistent, and persistent. Upon the birth of her own son, the daughter of this family considered the meaning of such procedures: what it had done to the father and to the children. She reacted against it, and determined to create very different ritualistic symbols in her own home.

Family Continuity

Previous descriptions of rituals have indicated their use in instilling ideas of the individual's relation to an immediate group. Other types of rites found in students' papers tended, in turn, to define that immediate group relatively. These show to the child that his own family circle is but the living link in a chain of generations that composes "the family." This concept of the family is important to the individual not only in respect to his own sense of worth and security, but also in respect to his attitudes toward responsibility for the future of the family. The American biological family unit has often been related, by scholars, to lack of long-range family responsibility. It is rather surprising, then, that thirty-five of the eighty-six students described rituals whose definite purpose it was to secure the ties between generations. (a) Ten of these told of family gatherings once a year in which every living member of the kinship group was invited to attend. Several were of the formal Family Reunion type, in which cases a public room was hired to accommodate the group, family business was discussed, minutes taken, and procedures published in pamphlet form. At a Family Reunion the program for the day usually includes announcements of births, deaths, outstanding activities, and honors, as well as addresses about origins, traditions, and famous ancestors. (b) Twenty-two students had smaller but formalized family gatherings upon stated holidays "to catch up with each other." (c) Three mentioned festive Sunday breakfasts each week, the meal at which married siblings always returned home with their spouses and children to discuss family affairs and to tell what had happened during the week.

These three types of rites, all of which served the same basic purpose and represent progressive steps in simplification of outward form, illustrate excellently the general trend of change in modern family rituals. The Family Reunion is an elaborate procedure somewhat comparable to the tribal gathering, with some pageantry, a special time at comparatively wide intervals, a certain public place, considerable advertising, a large personnel, and "ruling elders"—the committee—to keep the rites according to custom. Its purposes are clear to the committee, and there is a conscious attempt at symbolism and indoctrination. The ritual impresses because it is highly organized, spectacular, and an event apart from ordinary life. The holiday family gatherings are less formalized, more restricted in personnel, have hosts rather than a committee, and are more frequent. The Sunday breakfast rites are still more frequent, but less formalized and populous. If there is a tribal elder, it is just "Grandma." Obviously the visible symbol of family continuity is considerably attenuated, but the frequency, subtle simplicity, intimacy, usualness, and democratic nature of this last rite has its own impressing power.[13] This suggests a reason why modern family rituals need to be studied in themselves, and not merely passed off as very weak survivals of older forms.

Family Cultural Origin

Closely related to the idea of continuity fostered through family ritual was that of cultural origin. Though the group under study was too homogeneous to be very revealing in this respect, certain signs appeared. Traditional rituals, such as celebration of the Passover; baking Pfeffernüsse and Springerle for Christmas distribution; the periodic gathering to sing Welsh songs and tell Welsh folk tales; the observing of Three Kings Day all served to remind children of their Jewish, German, Welsh, or Latin American cultural heritage, and to preserve certain identifying marks of that heritage.

Summary

If one reviews only the few rituals noted in this study, one can see how large a part of individual personality and behavior is represented. A thumbnail sketch of a man could be drawn on the basis of his behavior and attitudes toward work, play, leisure, sex, illness, religion, affectional response, etiquette and social graces, responsibility for future generations, etc. Carrying this consideration one step farther, it can be seen what may be the results to subsequent home life from the combining of two ritual systems. A bride, for instance, who had long looked forward with pride to the time when she could call in her own husband on baking day to "lick the bowl," as the men of her family had always done, was reduced to tears and prolonged resentment when her groom responded "What? That raw stuff!" Superficial as it may appear, this sort of thing, as well as whether to vacation separately or together, to send the children to camp or not, how to celebrate Christmas and

[13] For an evaluation of this process as it affects contemporary rites of passage, see Bossard, *op. cit.*, pp. 427-531.

Sunday, who does the dishes and the shopping, how one behaves at meals, are not things that are frequently reasoned
out before marriage. They are patterns unconsciously *expected*
and raise emotional temperatures when observed differently.
They become even more important when there are children to
be considered, and each parent wants them to perform the
"right" way. For these reasons, a careful analysis of family
rituals, so individualized and so obscure in the modern family,
seems a significant part of the study of that group.

It should be repeated that in this discussion of the influence
of family ritual upon children and their development there
has been no attempt to suggest sole causation of specific effects.
It is all too obvious that a single critical event may completely
turn the course of conditioning set by rituals, and further, that
rituals themselves are, for the most part, just the channelizing
of certain deep-seated desires and attitudes into habitual behavior patterns. The hypothesis of this study has been merely
that: (1) the ritual is a means of communicating overtly the
ways of doing things and the attendant attitudes that a family
has found to be most satisfactory for its own use; (2) this
ritual behavior is practiced repeatedly, unchanged, and is
largely unconsciously performed; (3) it covers many aspects
of family life which are inescapable from it, and will continue
in the next generation of the family; (4) rituals symbolizing
the same phases of life are observed very differently from
family to family and are a part of what makes individuals
noticeably different from each other; and (5) these individual
differences, as crystallized in, and influenced by, rituals are
just as significant as comparisons of ritualistic differences from
primitive to civilized cultures, or from one national culture
to another.

5

Some Trends in Family Ritual: 1880-1946

$\mathbb{S}$INCE 1880, a group of strangers has arrived to join hands and circle the American home: automobiles and plumbing, radios and movies, big cities and small houses, public schools and cheap printing processes are some of their names. The family has opened its door wide to welcome part of them into the family circle and to greet others as nonresident relatives. But with their acceptance, just as with the arrival of a new baby, the family status quo is upset, and home life has to be rearranged. One kind of change that takes place is in family rituals: a family's prescribed, formal ways of meeting certain situations because these ways have come, through experience, to be the most satisfactory ones in that home. When a new element changes the family composition, these habitual forms tend to become modified.

Many such modifications appeared while comparing groups of family rituals practiced before World War I with those in use since that time. The changes indicated in this study are suggested by comparing the rituals found in a hundred published autobiographies, in which the period of childhood represented was largely from 1880 to 1917, with ones described by eighty-six university students whose rituals extended from 1917 to 1946. The nature of the experiment is merely exploratory and postulative, for the two groups studied are individually selective and not mutually comparable: their only points of identity being that all cases are roughly average or above average in economic status and education. Nevertheless, trends in family rituals appeared that are so marked as to be deemed worthy of recording if only as a stimulus to further investigation. The most noticeable of these trends will be described.

Education

Before the days when compulsory education led to easy accessibility to public and private schools, many children were taught at home during the early years. In the homes of autobiographers whose parents were well-to-do, there was often a nursery schoolroom with desks, blackboard, and a governess presiding. A stated period of every weekday was spent there in learning lessons: each child going through the same programs that had been visited upon his older siblings. In homes less affluent, the parents themselves took on the children's education. Usually it was Mother who set aside a certain time after breakfast to teach them. Sometimes it was Grandmother or a maiden aunt who took over the role of schoolmistress as her contribution for living with the family. However it was performed individually, the ritual was obligatory, formalized, and an integral part of family life. After children started going out of the home in great numbers for their schooling, parents did not quickly forego their usual ways. The traditional family schoolroom ritual was modified to meet the new situation. Early evenings, after dinner, found many families of children seated around the dining-room table, a lamp in the center, and their books in front of them, while Mother, with her sewing basket on her lap, "heard their lessons." In some homes, in lieu of this, question-and-answer games were devised during dinner hour, so that Father could supervise the school progress of the children. Gradually there appeared a school on every other block and a radio in every home. The new 1950 textbook is no longer the classic with which Mother and Father are familiar. And so a general evening ritual in the students' families seems to be an early family gathering around the radio, with children doing their lessons singly, in study periods at school, or in their own rooms. What remains of the original school-room ritual is, as a rule, nothing more than the monthly report-card session at home: a rather awesome occasion when Mother or Dad looks over each card, comments, criticizes, and hands out privileges and penalties. The trend from emphasis on family coöperative education to a demand for good marks for the sake of family reputation is apparent in the rituals of these groups.

Reading

Closely associated with the above rites are reading rituals. Since early education was at home, and books were few and expensive, families usually purchased only the best, according to their estimates, and used them over and over again as part of the education and recreation rites in their homes. This meant reading aloud to small children; and the babies could not be pampered with easy reading because all ages were present and had to use the same books. A large part of this reading was the classics and the Bible. *Pilgrim's Progress* was a favorite for Sunday reading. Dickens and Thackeray and their ilk were prominent during weekday evenings. History, Latin, and Greek were popular. In few instances were periodicals or newspapers read to the children. These reading-aloud rituals were not discontinued when the children learned to read, for by that time the ritual was pleasing in itself, and the material read was not outgrown, but suited to all ages. The ritual survived during the lifetime of the autobiographers' families, and the literature became a cherished part of the cultural possessions of the growing boys and girls. Today's students reveal a vast difference. Though many parents read aloud to the babies in the family before bedtime, and it is a cherished rite at that time, books especially designed for tots are cheap and plentiful. These and the "funnies" are the usual choices for such occasions.

By the time Johnny is six and going to school, the books read to the baby are just "kid stuff" to him. He disengages himself from the rite, and when the baby in turn goes to school the ritual is discontinued. Few contemporary university students mentioned any reading aloud in their families except for devotional Bible reading, and reading the Sunday funnies to younger siblings. Their most prominent reading ritual was the family gathering daily to read silently the morning or evening newspaper. The classics themselves did not give birth to more rigid formulae than are described by students concerning the place, time, regulations, and privileges surrounding their daily newspaper-reading rituals.

Bathing and Dressing

The Saturday night bath used to be a real occasion and not just a subject of humor. Actually it often took place regularly on Saturday afternoon or Sunday morning, simply because it meant sitting naked in three or four inches of water heated on a stove, and it was taken when the house was comparatively warm. It had to be at the end of the week, however, because it was a symbol of washing off the grime of labor and the week's sins, to be ready for an immaculate fresh start on Sunday. It was a whole family affair, often involving Father's bringing in the water to heat, and Mother's supervising the baths of the children from the oldest to the youngest in order, before the parents themselves went through the rite of purification. The order was important in that the weekly change of stockings and underwear and the donning of "best clothes" accompanied this rite. Children were not allowed to play once this transformation took place, and the baby was least able to sit still for long. He therefore was bathed last of the children. The symbolism of this ritual was very striking as author after author described the family feelings of renewed cleanliness and righteousness as they assembled fresh-washed and arrayed in their best clean clothes. When privileged families began to install indoor piping for water and heat, the bathtub and furnace took away from this ritual most of its hard-labor aspects, but did not immediately change the whole rite nor its significance. The Saturday night bath came into its own as a solemn ritual between Mother and the children. The evening was appropriate because the house was warm enough now, and the children could pop into bed and stay clean for Sunday morning. Since the new plumbing did away with the necessity for all to bathe at once, Father sometimes postponed his weekly bath till Sunday morning. That the spirit of the rite remained, however, can be seen in one author's description of how Father every Sunday morning at breakfast, fresh from the tub, looked over his children, scrubbed the night before and, said "*I'm* the cleanest member of the family!" With the facilities, the standards of cleanliness went up. Standards have even seemed to outstrip the facilities in students' homes. For now, according to them, the baby has to wait to be bathed each day until the rest of the family is out of the way, and family bathroom ritual chiefly concerns order of occupancy and allotment of time for possession. It symbolizes family order and thoughtfulness, merely assuming that all must be presentably clean at all times. For children of "dating" age, the bathroom is often reserved in the early evening, while the rest own it at times appropriate to their convenience. The clean clothing is still a part of the rite, but its symbolism is more secular. In very formalized homes, the before-dinner bath is a necessary prologue to "dressing for dinner." In others, it accompanies "putting on a dress for dinner" (in lieu of slacks, jeans, and housecoats).

The Sunday Drive

A ritual that seems to have lost none of its appeal for families since 1880 is the Sunday afternoon drive. Its meaning, however, has changed fundamentally. The autobiographers told of their drives together after Sunday dinner as being symbols of family pride and self-consciousness. In open carriages, with horses especially groomed, and the family clean, well-dressed and righteous after their morning in church, the little tribe drove out to parade in a brief circuit traversed by similar equipages of their neighbors. It was the family at its best, on show, up for comparison with the families of their friends. Today's students, who write frequently and with as much pleasure about their Sunday drives, crowd into a low-hooded automobile where they can hardly be seen, and cover as many miles as they can in the hours allotted for the ride. The family is alone among strangers, escaping together the week's routine, seeing new sights, and having relaxing fun.

Home Entertainment

Autobiographers' families had to entertain themselves, for there was often nowhere else to go, or no means of going elsewhere. Satisfying experiments became ritualized and were a formal part of home life. Reading aloud was one such entertainment, but families also organized musical evenings which were family concerts, family plays, family newspapers, Bible bees, spelling bees, and many other family-invented games for special times of the week or year. It was all in the nature of active participation, and usually competitive. Today, in spite of the fact that there are many other places than home to find entertainment, the students' families still find it pleasant to have certain set periods for family entertainment at home. But why write a family paper when one is delivered at the door each day? Why organize a play when one can hear the Lux Theater? Why go through long hours of practicing to make up a mediocre family orchestra when one can take out Rachmaninoff's own recording of his Second Piano Concerto, or hear Vaughn Monroe at will? There is a hint that Sunday night is becoming family night chiefly because of certain radio programs. Other programs during the week draw some families together unfailingly, and the home library of records has produced stated evenings for family concerts. These latter rites are different from the former in at least three respects: the material involved is broader in scope and the performance is professional rather than amateur; participation is passive; and there is seldom any competition involved.

The Evening Snack

Not only have old rituals become modified in the modern family, but new ones have been instituted. Several of these were so frequent in students' papers as to merit attention. The evening snack is one such ritual. In the autobiographers' stories, the day ended early. As soon as the lessons or the evening recreation was completed, the children were sent off to bed and the parents followed. Nine and ten o'clock were the times mentioned when the day was definitely over. After all, the family had been together for most of the day, often at all three meals, and had worked pretty hard. They were tired, talked out, and ready to separate. In the students' homes, frequently no member of the family sees any other member from breakfast till dinnertime, and after dinner adolescent children often go their own ways while Mother and Dad visit friends or the movies. Even if they spend the evening together with the radio, victrola, playing cards, or at the movies, there is little chance for just talk. Talk interferes with such activities. All this leads to a ritual that seems to be growing into a sort of fourth daily meal: a family gathering in the kitchen before bedtime for a snack. Naturally this rite includes only adolescent children and their parents, but it has an especially deep significance for them in that it becomes an opportunity for family council in an atmosphere even more intimate and democratic than that of the formal family dinner table. Here one relates to the family all that has happened during the day, and gets it off one's chest before going to bed. Members catch up with each other, give advice, solve problems, and perhaps go to bed feeling that though one has been alone all day, and will be tomorrow, one really has a family after all. The way in which students describe this rite reveals that it is highly valued in fulfilling some such purpose.

Doing the Dishes

Gone are the days when children were kept busy during every waking moment performing their necessary part of the family household business enterprise. Gone, too, is the era described by some autobiographers when even a family with modest means included enough hired help or dependent relatives to free the children from household tasks. Now, in most homes, there is actually a need for some help from children, but the children themselves are so busy that to catch their interest and instruct them is more trouble than it is worth. Doing the dishes after dinner seems to be a concession to this situation that many families make. It suits the children because it is really not very hard work, it comes at a time of day that does not ordinarily interfere with other activities, and it is "showy" work. Furthermore, it is actually valuable, for Mother is tired from the day's routine and to have company and assistance in the kitchen is very gratifying. Therefore a sense of importance and family coöperation can come through this performance even to children who criticize it bitterly. Some students' families make an efficient routine of it, each member having a specific chore, with special arrangements for "nights off" or for speeding the process on "movie night." Some play games during the dishwashing. Another makes it a ritual to sit at table over-long complaining about the chore ahead, but all the time enjoying the idea of obligatory family enterprise during this one time each day. Students showed considerable pride in their part in this family ritual, writing as if they were assured that through this performance they were fulfilling a part of their responsibility for the smooth functioning of the household.

Walking the Dog

Fido has his own contribution to make in the way of current American family rituals. In the autobiographies, stories about animals appeared often, but they were seldom household pets. They lived outdoors or in the barn. Fido ran at large and did not have to be walked. In modern urban dwellings there is no place for Fido except in the house, and if he is allowed to run at liberty he is an abomination to the neighbors. This has brought about the ritual, very prominent in students' papers, of walking the dog. It is an occasion of rigid obligation. The time is set and certain. The dog himself knows his part, and sometimes brings the leash to the proper person at the proper time. The personnel must be dependable. Often the actual walking is delegated to one person, but other services such as feeding, the daily romp, putting to bed, bathing, clipping are doled out amongst the family members. These procedures have to be well ritualized or Fido is upset for he is only an animal who is supposed to operate at the level of habit. But these family pet rituals are not just a necessary responsibility for the families. Fido himself has a new meaning in family life. He can be more of a person in his own right now because there are fewer persons in the family. Furthermore, he is the baby who never grows up, to substitute for the ever-present baby in the old-fashioned family. He is, then, an extra affectional tie where ties are few; a dependent one; and one who needs special consideration because his own normal way of living has been so curtailed by what humans have made of the modern world. Dog-lovers may question whether Fido is more important now than he has ever been. But the cases under study at least indicate that he is more often intimately included in the family rituals as a proper family member.

Present-giving

Autobiographers mentioned Christmas and birthdays as the times when elaborate present-exchanging took place in their homes. Lists of wants were kept for a whole year against these special events. Students' families found many more excuses to create such occasions. In some, all holidays meant exchanging gifts, and in others there was a weekly ritual involving such a procedure. In one family the children never went to the corner store, the city, or on a trip without bringing home a gift for Mother. In another the baby always met Mother at the door upon her return home with the confident question "What's you brang me?" Obviously there is much more opportunity and stimulus to buy gifts today than there was formerly. Money is handed out to children more freely, and attractive merchandise in reality or in picture presses upon one everywhere. But this in itself is, perhaps, not sufficient motivation for so much rigid ritual. Students of ritual processes have said that present-giving is a symbol of subordination, of tying oneself, through favor, to a necessary person. The exchanging of gifts makes this relationship alternately mutual. If this be so, it can be readily seen why the ritualistic exchanging of gifts is so important in a modern family where affectional ties are few and comparatively intermittent. In such cases it becomes more than sarcasm to say: "It is not the intrinsic value of a thing . . ."

The Family Meal

Modern city life has had a marked effect on the family meal, if our cases are representative. Autobiographers, most of whom lived in relatively rural settings, described mealtimes as three unavoidable daily periods of family refueling. They were of equal importance to the physical man, even though dinner, which usually came at noon, more formally met the requirements of the social man, No regular family meal that was not highlighted because of a birthday or holiday was an "occasion," for mealtime came around again relentlessly a few hours after the last one. It was a family meal every time, even the father often being at home in the middle of the day to share it. Furthermore, there appeared to be just two sacrosanct places for eating: the kitchen and the dining room.

Our present-day ritual recorders are largely city people. As will be seen in Chapter 6, breakfast is a meal which is fitted into the shortest possible period between a delayed getting out of bed and a rush to be on time for school or work. It has its rigid ritual procedures, chiefly of an efficiency and time-saving nature, but it is not a time for family gathering *per se*. At noontime there is "something to eat" for whoever happens to be at home; but once the children are of school age, Mother is frequently the only one left at home, and she seems to prefer to "pick up a bite" which will sustain her but interfere as little as possible with her other activities. The considerable increase in the giving of luncheons by the urban and suburban married-woman set has probably resulted in large part from this situation.

Weekday dinnertime—always in the evening for our current cases—is therefore an "occasion"; the first meal of the day when the family is all together and at comparative leisure. It rings with a warm, festive tone that was not heard in the earlier cases. There is considerable experimenting with the setting of the meal. In spring, summer, and fall, families try out a porch, or build a barbecue and take to the lawn, not just for company picnics but for regular family dinners. In winter there are card-table meals around the fireplace on certain nights. These settings add to the feeling of family reunion at the end of the day and make dinner extra special.

Though autobiographers mentioned Sunday breakfasts and dinners as "different," the atmosphere was distinctly holy. Meals were as they were on that day because there was church to be attended and the Sabbath to be kept sacred. Today our writers speak of Sunday breakfast as *the* breakfast of the week, with special menus, no need to get up early, no school or work to rush toward, the whole family together, often in robes and slippers. Joy in this particular meal superseded that over Sunday dinner, which often becomes very informal, catering to the mood of a day of rest—but not in the scriptural sense of that term.

The autobiographers' only occasion for missing a meal at home was to dine at a friend's house, and therefore was outside the range of regularized family ritual. In the modern family, dining out is a true family rite, though it occurs in a restaurant. Many families adhere to this once-a-week ritual, year after year, having one set night to eat out, and either one steadily patronized restaurant or a system of wide-range exploring.

Community-provided Family Rituals

Commercialized recreation and community activities have created a new opportunity for variety and frequency of family rituals outside the home. When the autobiographers went out together as a family, which they did seldom as compared to current practice, it was to take a drive, a walk, to visit friends, go to a "social," see an occasional play, or hear a concert. Today, unto all these have been added: movies, sports events of all kinds, local fairs, circuses, holiday parades, advertising "shows," the department store Santa Claus, each of which is the core of some family rites in our case studies. According to the autobiographers, commercial recreation was regularized as family ritual at the rate of once or twice a year. In current case studies, once a week is most usual. "A day downtown" (Saturday) has become a regular family rite which sometimes includes a number of the above-mentioned activities in the one day. Frequently the evening out is celebrated in conjunction with the restaurant dinner, giving freedom from cooking and dishwashing, and a more general spirit of celebration. Daytime rites of this sort begin when children are quite young; others, when the children are old enough to keep awake all evening. In some families these regular practices become so honored that even when children are in mid-adolescence they cling to the family day or evening in preference to joining social activities with their own friends at those times. In other cases, this sort of rite passes into the keeping of Mother and Dad who, no doubt with mixed regret and pleasure, are patronized into a "Mother's and Dad's day out" by their children.

Father-child Ritual Schedules

In the homes of autobiographers, Father (as well as the family meal) was somewhat like the poor, whom "we have always with us." He is so no longer. He is so seldom present during the normal course of weekday family life that if he is to spend much time being fatherly he must almost of necessity catch his children from out their own routines and activities and make appointments with them. This has led to father-child ritual schedules, from the infant level on up through adolescence. Father spends a certain time with the babies, before or after dinner, during which time regular pastimes are invented. The weekly family outing is arranged at a time when he can be present. As children grow older, he and the boys go off to a game once a week, or have a fishing or camping trip once or twice a year. Girls too have regular special occasions with Dad, from which Mother is often rigidly excluded —movie nights, shopping trips, Saturday or Sunday golfing. Some children we have shown in earlier chapters greeting the transient family member with a cocktail, fruit juice, slippers, the newspaper upon his return each day. Dad was also seen presiding over dishwashing as a deliberate ruse for weekly family council with the boys. These types of activities shared by father and children are not all new. Many of them were common in autobiographers' homes. What *is* new is the increasing approach to formalizing the time, place, content of all these father-child relationships in order to assure some definite communication where that communication might otherwise be infrequent and haphazard.

Summary

A comparison of family rituals popular before the first World War with those in use since shows certain changes which seem to run parallel to changes in family environment brought about with modern industrialism.

1. Mass production education has taken the schoolroom and homework rituals out of the home, and left, for the most part, a mere periodic family checking-up on report cards. Mass production publishing and printing has helped to wipe out family evenings of reading the classics aloud and has substituted instead a bedtime reading of child literature to the babies and a silent, but companionable daily newspaper rite for the whole family.

2. Modern heating and plumbing and new standards of fastidiousness have completely changed the ritual of the Saturday night bath—a symbol of Godliness in cleanliness—to a daily procedure stressing orderliness and mutual thoughtfulness.

3. With the advent of mass production automobiles, the Sunday drive has become a family conspiracy for escape and

variety, rather than a horse-and-carriage open show of family pride to well-known neighbors.

4. The regular evening at home, at present, ritualizes largely around the radio and the record player, with family behavior regulated, but passive and non-competitive. Formerly, family evenings were family-invented amateur programs, involving active participation in games and projects.

5. Certain new rituals have arisen as needs are felt because of the family separation caused by modern techniques and ways of living. One of these is the evening snack, at which parents and adolescents who have been apart from each other all day engage in informal family council. Another is the formalized dish-washing rite, often the single opportunity for family-shared work and responsibility.

6. The family dog has come into his own as a participant in family rituals, not only because, in urban life, he must be kept in the house and "walked" at intervals; but also because he is often a substitute for the ever-present baby in the former larger family.

7. Family present-giving rituals have increased in number and formality. High-pressure advertising is a large factor in creating them; the symbolic meaning of gift-giving is also important in the family where affectional ties are few and physical closeness sporadic.

8. Weekday breakfasts and lunches have declined as family rites and have assumed the aspect of necessary but inconvenient interludes between other pressing activities. Dinner, however, has been accented as a festive reunion meal, and Sunday breakfast as an extended and leisurely one. No longer is the setting for the family meal confined to kitchen or dining room. A seasonal change of setting may occur within the house and out in the yard. A public restaurant often becomes a setting away from home.

9. Commercialized recreation and community activities, readily available just around the corner, have created an essentially new kind of family ritual; the regular day or evening out.

In its frequency and variety of content it is strikingly different from anything found in the records of an earlier period.

10. A ritualistic "schedule of appointments" between father and children is seen emerging in current case studies. This is interpreted as resulting from the decrease in the time during which they are both at home together, and from an attempt to assure some periods of definite father-child relationships.

11. All of these comparisons of family rituals, 1880 to 1946, are generalized from the specific case material of this study. Many of them seem more generally applicable on the basis of common-sense observation. Projection beyond this case material, however, is in question form only, awaiting further materials for the answers.

Class Differentials in Family Rituals

SOCIAL CLASS is a concept not to be lightly approached in contemporary America. To use the term in ordinary social conversation is usually considered bad taste. When the subject cannot be avoided, a well-worn technique is to pronounce the word "class" with an exaggeratedly broad *a*, suggesting total lack of sympathy with such divisions. In academic fields, social class is a concept popular among social scientists. But they too must be prepared for attack from colleagues who insist that up to the present no one really knows what social class is, or what are the factors and variables which separate one social class from another. Until these are definitely ascertained, a student who attempts to place cases in a class category runs the risk of being thought a self-appointed Saint Peter determining who should enter, or be expelled from, the Pearly Gates. Yet in spite of the verbal quarantining of social class, and the insistence that its determinants are still unknown, the phenomenon itself is a functioning reality. Few people are unaware of its pervasive actuality, and many use it for their own purposes. Were the students of family life to await the ultimate refinements of class measurements, they would be neglecting too long an important segment of family culture which has great significance, even when based upon tentative and unscientific definitions of class that are nevertheless functioning definitions in the mind of the public as it lives its everyday life.

In the Philadelphia metropolitan area, for instance, from which most of the case material in this chapter was obtained, it is obvious to a native son that at least three social classes exist and are generally acknowledged. Certain communities are spoken of as upper-, middle-, or lower-class communities. This is often a factor in choice of home sites. Some non-residential streets also have such acknowledged status. In the downtown business section, the three parallel main streets, Market, Chestnut, and Walnut, are thought of by old-timers as being lower-, middle-, and upper-class hunting-grounds. Even these streets are subdivided vertically, so that the western section has generally higher social status than the eastern section.

However these ratings may have been originally determined, many agents purposely cater to them and thereby strengthen them. Architects and builders know the most potent selling features for houses in different kinds of communities, though costs of the houses may be substantially the same. Buyers for stores consider, in terms of their particular clientele, the needs, habits, and tastes which they know vary markedly amongst the classes —a consideration quite separate from that of mere price differences. The success of commercialized recreation depends, to a great extent, upon its location and recognition of different class habits. Public acknowledgment of these differences is evident also in the city newspapers, and particularly in Sunday editions, where a survey of advertisements, news items, and reports of social events clearly reveals an attempt to group together the information of interest to one "set" or another. From one limited point of view, the city can be seen as organized around the recognized fact of social class.

The Meaning of Social Class

Because of the subjective values placed upon class membership, it is comforting to many people to consider economic differences as synonymous with class differences. If this were the case, a family could easily be placed on the social ladder by an inspection of its income in relation to its needs. The influence of social class upon children would be largely in terms of what money buys for them that makes their life different from others'; and financial gains or reverses would automatically change the family's or individual's social position. The untruth of this has been recognized by aspiring parents of growing children, by realistic novelists, and by students who prefer to examine life before theorizing about it. The latter, therefore, have made attempts at approaches to the study of class other than the economic one.[1]

For the purposes of this chapter, the approach to social class is best defined as follows:

"A social class, properly understood, is a cultural reality. Approached scientifically, its identification is not an academic exercise in snobbery or a subjective evaluation, but a recognition of the fact that people live and work and play and think at different levels. The differences between classes are not merely financial or ostentatious; they encompass the entire range of social behavior—occupation, consumption habits, education, manner of speaking, mode of dress,

[1] For a discussion of these approaches and a brief summary of class differentials and their general significance in child development, the reader is referred to James H. S. Bossard, *The Sociology of Child Development*, New York, Harper & Brothers, 1948, chapter XIII. For a more complete discussion of the contemporary concept of social class and its role in American life, consult W. Lloyd Warner and Paul S. Lunt, *The Social Life of a Modern Community*, New Haven, Yale University Press, 1941, For further information on procedures in analyzing social classes see W. Lloyd Warner, Marchia Meeker, and Kenneth Eels, *Social Class in America*, Chicago, Science Research Associates, 1949. For a study of the impact of social classes on adolescents in a middle western community, see A. B. Hollingshead, *Elmtown's Youth*, New York, John Wiley & Sons, Inc., 1949. For a general study of class in an American community see W. Lloyd Warner and Associates *Democracy in Jonesville*, New York, Harper & Brothers, 1949.

philosophy of life, recreational pursuits, associational activity, social attitudes, family life, and the like."[2]

Within the boundaries of social class, thus described as a cultural reality, lies the subject of family ritual, a patterning of family behavior. It is to an investigation of how these rituals may vary from class to class that this chapter is devoted.

The Case Material

The attempt here is to discover how family rituals vary among social classes, and not to investigate how many class subdivisions exist, or what are their determinants. The families under study therefore, are placed in only three class categories —middle, lower, and upper—described above as being functioning class categories. Further division would tend only to obscure meaning in a limited investigation.

Two problems presented themselves in collecting material for this purpose. (a) The cases, individually, had to be recognizable by some standard as belonging to one of these three classes. This problem was attacked by approaching families who lived in neighborhoods, used services, had occupations, and belonged to institutions that are, to Philadelphians, unequivocally lower, middle, or upper class. It seemed important to select, from these, cases in which the individual's ratings of themselves agreed with public conception of their class status, and in which there could be no question of their being marginal, or of belonging to more than one class. Some examples of sources for obtaining interviews were: settlement houses; a community in which most of the women are employed in domestic service; a public school in a middle-class suburban district; a private school catering to the debutante set; the Junior League; etc.[3] (b) There had to be reasonable distribution of cases among the three classes. Case records already obtained,

[2] Bossard, *op. cit.*, p. 285.

[3] The authors are indebted to: Mrs. James M. Skinner, Regional Director of the Junior League of America; Miss Theodora Ninesteel; Miss Gertrude S. Butler; and Dr. T. E. M. Boll, for information and for help with interviews and questionnaires.

and described in preceding chapters, were used whenever class placement, as defined above, was possible. These being preponderantly middle class, new cases were collected to improve the distribution. One hundred and fifty-six cases (almost wholly Philadelphian, and collected through essays, questionnaires, and interviews, or all three) form the basis of this analysis. In each class there is represented the family ritual of children now fourteen years of age or over, as well as the childhood rituals of the present-day parent generation. To these cases are added the materials obtained from seventy-three published autobiographies. These are used only for purposes of comparison, and are so noted in the text, since they largely represent an earlier era and widely scattered locales.

The Physical Background

In the present study, the physical setting of the home in which the rituals occur appears to be an important factor, both in influencing the kinds of rituals instituted and in permitting an understanding of why they arise. Therefore a brief description of the general physical details of these homes at each class level is in order.

1. THE LOWER-CLASS HOME

The homes represented by the lower class range from a two-room apartment to a six-room house. In them live families of from four members to thirteen members. There is no positive correlation between size of home and size of family. A family of thirteen lives in a six-room house; so does a family of four. A family of eight lives in three rooms; one of seven in two rooms, and so forth, In no case does a family have more than one bathroom, and in some apartments one is shared with another family. The kitchen situation is similar: some families share basement kitchen facilities with others, or simply have a stove in the living room. Only the larger houses have a dining room which is reserved as such.

Within these confines, if there is one bedroom, it belongs to the parents, and often to several of the youngest children also. A second bedroom means that if a married sibling lives at home, this married couple and their children also have a separate room. With these preferences attended to, the rest of the children distribute themselves in other available bedrooms or throughout the house on cots, couches, etc.

2. THE MIDDLE-CLASS HOME

The middle-class family lives in a three-room apartment at one extreme, and in practically every size dwelling up to a twenty-two-room house at the other. Here there is definite correlation between rooms and family size. In all cases, the parents have a private bedroom which is not shared by any child past his first year. All children sleep in bedrooms, and when they share them, they do so only with siblings of the same sex. Most of the homes have dining rooms: some have kitchen-dinette or living-dining-room combinations. All homes have a private bath, usually one, or at most two, on the second floor, with an occasional extra in the basement, first floor, or third floor.

3. THE UPPER-CLASS HOME

These upper-class families do not live in apartments. They have houses of from sixteen to thirty rooms, and all with separate dining rooms. Children past nursery age each have their own bedrooms, and sometimes the parents have separate adjoining ones. In many cases, each member of the family has his own private bath; in all cases bathrooms are plentiful in relation to family size. There is not the frequent doubling-up with married relatives that occurs in the lower class, and less often in the middle class. In the only upper-class family in which a married sister lives with the parents, she (a divorceé with two children) has a completely separate apartment of her own within the house. Another factor, marking the upper-class home, is that in all but four of them there are from one to nine servants living in the house. These usually occupy the third floor, or an apartment off the kitchen quarters. Finally, many of these families have a second home to which they repair in summertime. Most of these, though less elaborate than the winter home, are not makeshift, rented cottages. They are established family homes.

The Rituals

I. DAILY PROCEDURES

There is a rhythm to everyday life which prevails quite generally throughout the families represented here—a rhythm which brings the members into interaction for a period during the morning, separates them for their individual activities, and brings reunion toward the close of the day. The two periods of family mingling entail certain necessary routines (waking, bathing, dressing, eating, etc.) that have to be repeated every day, and therefore are apt to fall into ritualistic forms, invariable and expedient. In some cases, the mere expediency makes them inviolable. In others, they also offer emotional satisfaction as the eternally dependable patterns characteristic of home, the certainties which always precede a new day of uncertainties, and to which one can return again after it.

There arises again the question whether some of the family procedures here described, particularly those of the lower-class families, fall properly into the category of ritual. Reference to the basic problem involved was made in Chapter II. According to Benedict, ritual by "accepted usage of the term does not include acts of routine provision of physical necessities. . . . Ritual is always extra-necessitous from the technological point of view."[4] On this point, we find ourselves in agreement with Krech and Crutchfield that "this distinction is of doubtful psychological validity."[5] To confine ritual to extra-necessitous forms of group behavior would be to restrict it largely to areas of leisured living which, from the standpoint of this study, would eliminate all, or nearly all, lower-class family rituals. The realities of lower-class living do not permit many extra-

---

[4] Ruth Benedict, "Ritual," the *Encyclopedia of the Social Sciences,* New York, The Macmillan Co., 1934, Volume 13, p. 396.

[5] David Krech and Richard S. Crutchfield, *Theory and Problems of Social Psychology,* New York, McGraw-Hill Book Co., Inc., 1948, p. 393.

necessitous forms of family behavior. *Right* and *rigid* forms of family procedure based on expediency seem to us to be as ritualistic as the extra-necessitous elaborations which emerge from more leisured living especially when the contemporary secularization of ritual is kept in mind.

Different ways of life, however, even within this general rhythm, lead to varied procedures. When these families are divided into three classes, similarity of rites within classes and differences between them are marked. One aspect of these three ways of life may, at the outset, explain a good deal about certain variations in the rituals to be described. In these middle-class families, school and business hours coincide very closely. For the most part all the family must be up together at the same time, and leave home at nearly the same time. In a home not cramped but not spacious either, this leads to one specific type of situation. In upper- and lower-class homes, on the contrary, the members' schedules do not coincide so closely. The business hours of Father and working children are often at very different times, and school hours at yet another. In the lower-class home, cramped for space, this has one meaning: in the upper, with separate rooms and with servants, quite another. Under such different circumstances, the degree of comfort to be attained by remaining at home as long as possible, or by getting away from it at the first practicable moment, also enters into the ritual picture. The following differences in rituals are in part results of these varied situations in the three classes.

A. Awakening

From this study it would seem that the alarm clock is the modern American equivalent to "the first crowing of the cock," by which it was decreed that the ancient Chinese family must arise. Some one person in most of these homes is awakened by the alarm, and it then becomes his duty to set off the daily morning procedures.

In the lower-class home, this person is most frequently the father, who has to leave home even before the young babies are clamoring for attention. Upon his departure the baton is passed to the mother, who clock-watches for each other member of the family with a schedule to meet.[6]

In the middle-class family, a parent usually supervises the alarm clock, and it is a signal for a rapid succession of awakenings, well routinized according to time limits beyond which each member may not be permitted to remain in bed. It is in the middle-class family that there is found the practice of wakening with a kiss, a song, or some sort of familiar family game or by-play.

The upper-class family is more individualistic in its awakening. Sometimes a servant rises by the alarm, and notifies each family member at the appointed time. A call on the house phone, a tap at the door, a closing of the bedroom windows are all predetermined signs of the proper moment for getting up. The mother often takes this responsibility just as she does in the middle- and lower-class homes. But also, children who are past high school age have their own alarm clocks, and dependably rise by them.

B. Bathroom Procedures

The fact that the middle-class family rises almost together, and has few bathrooms, has resulted in a problem for it, which has been resolved by a very narrowly prescribed ritual for many of them—a bathroom ritual. They have developed set rules and regulations which define who goes first (according to who must leave the house first), how long one may stay in, what are the penalties for overtime, and under what conditions there may be a certain overlapping of personnel. It is usually required that actual tub-bathing be done the evening before. But a good wash and a toothbrushing, as well as a daily shave for the men, must be fitted into this precedence- and time-defined rite.

Upper-class girls, most of whom had their own individual

---

[6] This study did not happen to include families in which the father worked late afternoon shifts or night shifts. This would obviously lead to a different situation.

bathrooms, reacted with interest when told of middle-class procedures in this respect. The lower-class girls were amazed that such a thing was necessary. Probably privacy, which they had never had, and over-fastidiousness were not family values which made such arrangements important.

C. Breakfast Rituals

In the material gathered from autobiographies published by adults, every family of each class considered breakfast a family meal. In the case records the parent generation too, for the most part, observed this as a family rite. But from the present generation records, the American family breakfast seems to be fast dying out. Breakfast here is a peripatetic meal, eaten individually or in relays, in a rush, and with little service. There are several reasons why this may be so. (a) People stay up later at night than they did a generation or two ago. There is more to do at night. This being so, even a few minutes of extra sleep in the morning is precious. And, time schedules of members differing, family breakfast becomes a lesser value than sleep, a meal to be postponed till the last minute and not to be lingered over. (b) Breakfast can be prepared more easily, even by youngsters, nowadays, what with canned fruit juices, prepared cereals, chocolate milk, packaged melba toast, and instant coffee. (c) The day of having a "hired girl" live in, even in lower-class homes, is gone. Few even of the middle class have a servant actually living in the home. And when servants come in for the day, they are considered a nuisance at breakfast time, because it is easier not to be dependent upon them, and not to have to cater to their time requirements.

By the time a lower-class youngster in these families is old enough for school, he is quite well equipped to get his own breakfast and get himself off to school. From that time on he does so, standing in the kitchen and dodging around any other members of the family who may happen to be attending to their own breakfasts simultaneously. It is only the young babies, with their mother, who have any sort of table-breakfast.

Even the father, for the most part, gets what he wants on his way to early work.

Since the middle-class family usually rises in rapid succession, there is a very well-worked-out procedure. Mother goes into the kitchen first, and starts breakfast. She serves the family in relays, working between stove and table: first the father, then the school children, and then often sits down herself and has her own breakfast with the remaining pre-school children. This meal, usually in the kitchen, is short, brisk, and highly mobile. But the different relays do eat at table, have a regular table-setting, and often a semblance of family conversation.

Breakfast is a highly individual affair with the upper class as with the lower, but with these differences. The food is usually prepared by a servant, and is taken by each member from the refrigerator, the buffet, or is served individually when desired. It is almost always eaten in the dining room. For small children, the meal is more leisurely and settled. Mother, nurse, or maids take care of them, and if it is the sort of home that affords a mademoiselle and a nursery, the pre-school children eat there. In such homes, the children often eat all their meals in the nursery until they are old enough to cope with the formalized intricacies of the evening meal that exist in this kind of home.

Upper- and middle-class families frequently make up for this sort of weekday breakfast with a late, large spread on Sunday morning. All the family sits at table, and the Sunday newspapers are conspicuous. Often this occasion includes the weekly entertaining of married siblings and their families. Sometimes it is the weekly occasion for entertaining guests.

D. Leaving Notes

The period immediately after breakfast gives rise to a ritual common to both upper- and middle-class families: the reporting to the family as to one's whereabouts and one's activities during the day.

In the upper-class home it is considered polite and proper to give the family such information daily, and it is done in many homes by the leaving of notes in especially designated places, because personal communication in the early morning is not usual. Note exchange is also a custom of the middle-class home. But more often these exchanges are verbal, since the family members do see each other in passing. With both classes, this is definitely the time of the day for checking up between parents and children. No lower-class child interviewed had any such custom.

E. Dinner

Dinner, in the American family represented here, is definitely at night, as it was not so consistently in the families of the autobiographers of an earlier era. It is often, indeed, the first time that the entire family meets together during the day.

In the lower-class family, however, dinner is almost the same kind of meal as is breakfast. The mother, or an older sister, does prepare the food, but the rest of the family comes and takes it when and where they want to. Some of these families never have a meal sitting down with the whole family together except for Sunday dinner, which is considered a very special occasion. Even at this meal some families have to eat in relays, or in different rooms, because there is not room enough for all of them at a table. In the smaller families, where the family does eat together every night, they do so in the kitchen, with the "everyday" tableware, the dining room tending to be reserved for holiday, Sunday, and entertaining, when the best china is brought out for use.

Middle-class dinner involves very formal procedures. It is at a certain time, usually six or six-thirty. It is a meal at which the whole family sits around the table, for the most part in the dining room, and at which each member has a special place to sit. Features of it, generally, are two: there are assigned tasks for different members of the family, such as serving, carving, clearing the table and doing the dishes; and second, though the dinnertime equipment is too varied to describe specifically, it is usually more formal and impressive than for other meals.

Dinner for the upper class is later, at about seven or seven-thirty, and is much more formal as to appointments and service. In all but three homes, servants took over the complete preparation and serving of the meal. White damask, well-polished silver, flowers, candlelight, dinner china and glassware, and a completely leisure atmosphere describe the situation of this meal. No one moves away from the table during the meal, except Father, if he carves from the sideboard. Cocktails before dinner and after-dinner coffee in the living room are, in many cases, regular parts of the dinner ritual.

II. WORK AND RECREATION

Work and recreation rituals, in the middle- and lower-class homes, are intimately related to each other, and in this respect: the time and opportunities for regular family recreation depend to a large extent upon the smooth functioning of necessary household routine. There is a definite maneuvering between household chores and the time left over to devote to leisure-time activities.

It is the middle-class family that has many organized work rituals which, once regularized, free it for regular periods of family entertainment. Housecleaning, marketing, dishwashing, preserving, even hair-washing, automobile- and dog-washing, and garden care are got through by having a certain day and time, certain jobs for each member, and ways considered most "correct," because most efficient, for doing them. (Many of these rituals have been described in detail in previous chapters, and are merely listed here, since the emphasis is on the class differentials themselves.) These families then can regularize, and do, one night as "family movie night"; Sunday afternoons as the time for a ride together, or a visit to relatives or friends; an evening for games or music, or entertaining. The family at the radio in the living room for certain programs is a very popular rite, not only on Sunday evenings, but often several other times during the week. Certain news commentators are "musts" for the whole family every day. Saturday is definitely a day for recreation. When children are small, this means some kind of family frolic. But even with children of college age, some part of Saturday figures largely as the time when the whole family engages in some activity that is different from the spirit of the rest of the week. Going down town to lunch and the movies, or having friends in to dinner to a more than usually elaborate meal are the two most popular ways of celebrating Saturday in the present-generation middle-class homes.

Coöperative rites of a menial nature are practically nonexistent in the upper-class homes. Even the few families which have no servant living in the house have day's help to perform these duties. Sharing dishwashing is the only frequent rite of this sort mentioned. For a few it is every night, and for others on the servants' nights out. The upper class does have rigidly set times for family recreation of a specific kind, but it is more often outside the home than is the case with the middle class, which tends to outside recreation together only during weekends. Usual types of regular family participation in the upper class are these: the orchestra during the season; golf or tennis on Sunday in spring, summer, and autumn; a weekly or monthly visit to Grandmother's; beagling every Sunday; the theatre once a month; opera during the season; always the horse shows; the Orpheus Club; the Stagecrafters; charity bazaars; the Penn-Cornell Game. Season tickets for orchestra, theatre, and opera are fairly common to middle-class college students, but these affairs are attended individually or with friends, not within the family, as with the upper class. At home, for the upper class, there is: bridge once a week; television every night; playing the piano and singing once a week. And though there are some families that always listen to certain radio programs together, for the most part they like different ones. After all, each one has his own radio in his room. Saturday is very definitely a day for frolic, but not so often in family, as with the middle class. Many social obligations center around this day, but they are separated into children's obligations and parents' obligations.

Saturday has a sharply different meaning to the girls of the lower class. Saturday is housecleaning day. It meant the same thing to all the girls interviewed, though they came from different communities. Except in the smallest families, all the children old enough, and preferably girls, spend most of the day helping to clean up the house. If, and when, they are finished, they are free to amuse themselves separately. There are no times for family recreation together. Work and recreation interlock in this way: older children have certain nights when they stay at home each week to take care of the younger ones in order that their parents, or their mother and a married sister or friend, may go to a movie. This night is usually the one on which the local theatre has bank night and is giving away free gifts. Aside from this time, the children seek out their own fun, and away from home. There are no family games and entertainments at home. Even the radio is not a family affair. Teen-agers said that they had given up trying to compete with Father's news programs, and the youngest's adventure serials. There are just too many people of too many ages to use one radio together. There are too many people in a small space to gather together comfortably for any kind of games.

III. RELIGIOUS RITUALS

There are two kinds of religious rituals observed in these families. First, there are rituals in the home, such as grace at meals, family prayers, Bible readings, Sunday procedures, celebration of sacred days. Second, there is regular family participation in religious services outside of the home.

Important in the interpretation of religious rituals on a class basis is the analysis of the religious and denominational make-up of the cases under discussion. Families belonging to the upper class in this study are all Episcopal or Presbyterian, with the former predominating. There are no Catholic families in this group. The middle class is composed of every major denomination and Catholics, with no preponderance of any one. The lower class represents the Catholic faith overwhelmingly, though there are Methodists and Baptists represented. The religious affiliation of the three classes as represented here may be characteristic of the general class population. But until this is ascertained, it must be admitted that religious affiliation may here have an influence on the rituals which unduly differentiates them, since the Catholic church is more dominantly the guardian of religion than is the case with Protestantism. Even in middle-class families in this study, religious rituals in the home are less usual in Catholic families than in Protestant ones. With this suggestion that the sample may be uncharacteristic in religious make-up, the rituals are described as they were discovered.

A. At Home

It is the middle-class families here described that carry the torch of religion in the home, though they also represent all but one of the admitted agnostic families. Grace is frequently said at meals, and in many different forms. It is not something done on special occasions, but a form that children remembered as having always been in effect, and that was still occurring without question. Bedtime prayers are as common. Children were taught them by a parent as soon as they were old enough to talk, and they were "heard" each night, often kneeling, for many years, after which time a good proportion of the children continued them individually even on to college age. The most popular childhood prayer was "Now I Lay Me," in spite of the mental hygienists' warnings; and mothers who had learned this prayer are now still teaching it to their youngsters, without revision. It is only the middle-class family that has regular family prayers apart from bedtime prayers and grace. In this class only is there celebrated the old-fashioned type of Sunday, in which no toys, work, sewing, games, or cooking are permitted.

While the family was small, and the children young, the pattern for the lower class was similar to that of the middle class. But as it grew, these forms died out. The children interviewed "thought" that the babies still said their prayers, but were not certain. Grace is said often, on the occasions when dinner is formalized enough to permit of such a period. Some Catholic families have a form of simple altar tacked to a wall, with no specific procedures for its use. But this is all that could be construed as religious ritual in these homes.

Upper-class children were also taught bedtime prayers by a parent or a nurse. At the time of the interview, however, only three of the girls still said their prayers independently at night. One interviewee explained this in these terms. "Nurse, or Mademoiselle taught us our prayers, with the approval of our parents, and heard us as long as she put us to bed. After that, we were on our own." This quick giving up of the form may be related to a conspicuous absence of all other religious forms in the family. There is in these homes ample opportunity for grace at meals, but only four families observe it. There are no family prayers or Bible readings. The general attitude, whether a rationalization or not, is that anything deeply religious in nature is personal and intimate, and would be very embarrassing if indulged in openly in family life. It seems highly probable, from the comparison of these cases in the three classes, that though all the parents feel the responsibility for teaching religious rites to small childreu, the rites do not endure where there is no adult pattern to nourish them.

B. Sunday Church Services

Only the small families in the lower class go to church together regularly on Sundays. With the larger ones it is an individual affair, and there is much more pressure between the priest and the child than between the parent and the child. Members can, in these cases, attend mass at the most convenient hours, and many of them do so in relays, so that someone is always at home to preside over the babies and to take care of the important occasion of the week—Sunday dinner.

More than half of the middle-class families always go to church together on Sunday morning. Some always attend midweek services. Children go to Sunday school, and to young people's services on up through their teens. The Sunday services are times for special dressing up, and certain Sundays mean corsages for the ladies, or new hats. Sunday dinner in these families is prepared for and set at a time that will not interfere with anyone's going to church.

In the upper class, nearly half the families go to church together regularly on Sunday mornings, and this also involves special dressing for the occasion. But there are two marked differences between the upper and middle classes. Even the upper-class families who always go on Sundays are conspicuous by their absence at other services, that day or during the week. The children who go to Sunday school and young people's organizations drop out at early teen age. In the group there was one "younger sister" who was still going to Sunday school, and one teen ager who teaches a class. At a fairly early age, in this group, other social activities come to crowd out church activities. Most of these children are, at this time, preparing for a very intricate sort of adult social life. The other difference is this: all the families, even those who never go to church regularly, usually go together on Thanksgiving, Christmas, Easter, and during Lent. These services are compulsory to the upper-class families in this study as they are not to non-church goers of the middle class. It seemed clear that these are occasions of high social, rather than of just religious, importance. Everybody who is anybody will be there. In respect to regarding certain ceremonies at church as social duties, one girl interviewed said, interestingly enough, that though her family never goes to church in the wintertime, if she is visiting and her host goes to church, she, of course, goes along too.

IV. RITES OF PASSAGE

In contrast to the rites of religious participation already discussed, and in relation to church attendance as a religious or a social duty, the different class attitudes toward the church as a center for christening, confirmation, weddings, and funerals is of interest. Every single member of the upper class who was questioned felt it important that family members be christened, confirmed, married in church, and have a church funeral. One patriarch, who never went to church, donates liberally to an élite institution by check once a year, "just in case." The other two classes were far less dogmatic in their pronouncements concerning the necessity for these church ceremonies—with one exception. Even among admitted agnostics, there was a clinging to the feeling that a funeral should be in a churchly atmosphere, or at least that a minister should be at hand to say a few words in behalf of the deceased. One lower-class girl, who lived with twelve other people in a two-bedroom home, reported that the family had been saving up for a long time in order to be able to move to a house with three bedrooms. Suddenly her grandfather died. He lived down South, and none of the children had ever seen him. But the house money had to be given over to Father, for a dark suit (he had only work clothes), for carfare, and for funeral expenses for Grandfather.

Class wedding rituals as found in this study deserve mention in their own right. For upper-class girls, a church wedding and a reception at home are essential. These are occasions that demand the services of a social director, who advises, plans, and manages all the intricate ritual surrounding such celebrations, just as she does in the case of the début. Most upper-class families would not think of attempting such an affair without expert help. Many middle-class girls do not want church weddings, or even receptions, and there is no disgrace socially to "going off and getting married" so long as there is due notice to family and friends. Those who do want more elaborate celebrations often avail themselves of the advice such as is offered by department stores, jewelers, florists, and photographers, and coördinate the details by themselves. Some of them plan the whole affair themselves, with their families, though usually a caterer is necessary for a reception at home. The lower class does not go in for such public elaborateness. Marriage by a priest figures high. A new dress to be married in, and flowers for the bride, are essential. Often a "spread" for a few friends at home is desired. If more friends are invited than can be entertained at home, a public hall is hired. To this hall there is brought food prepared at home, of the potato salad, sliced meat, and beer variety. Even the invitations to weddings vary on a class basis. In Philadelphia stores selling such stationery there are to be found many different types, from the Emily Postian engraved invitation on heavy white or india paper, to the little card folder, fastened in front by two clasped hands and containing inside the words: "You are cordially invited to the joining in matrimony of —— and ——, at ——, on ——."

V. SUMMER VACATIONS

The summer vacation is becoming more individualized with the advent of easier and cheaper transportation and more freedom for young people. In published autobiographies, most families who could afford a vacation described a regular vacation ritual. A far lesser proportion of the present-day families did so. But with some it is still well established, and varies among the classes.

With the upper class, summer is the time when there is a transplanting of the family to a more favorable location. Usually this is a removal to a second home where, though it may be on a simpler scale, the same kinds of social relationships and activities are carried on as in the wintertime, and often with many of the same people, since people from the same winter communities cluster at the same resorts. Members may take trips abroad, or go on visits across the continent; but they do it from this summer center, where they all automatically go for the season. Newport was, of course, the grand model for this kind of resort,[7] and there are many of them, in descending scale of affluence and formality, which maintain rather tight little circles of social life. In one New Jersey resort, to which some of the families under study move each summer, there is one beach labeled as the "swank set beach." There are no

[7] For a description of the model of such resorts, see *Cleveland Amory*, "Newport: There She Sits," *Harper's Magazine*, February, 1948.

ordinances to prevent anyone from using it, yet no one but the "set" bathes therefrom. Sightseers walk through, but return to the other beaches for their swimming. The "set" has a quite separate social life, and does not mingle with others at the resort. Many of them own homes there, and appear at this beach year after year, beginning as small babies and ultimately appearing with their own offspring.

The middle-class vacation is not so predetermined, for they do not so often own a home just for summer use. There is a time in the year, however, when Father brings home a few road maps to plan the trip, or Mother goes to the shore or mountains to hire a cottage for the season or for a few weeks. If it is for the season, Father usually commutes over weekends, except during his own short vacation. The middle-class vacation is less often a transplanting of a community of friends, and more often a meeting of new and different people, or of the "regular summer friends." Life is lived on a much less formal scale, and is usually definitely planned to be very different from the winter regimen.

A week at the shore or at Grandmother's is the best that the lower-class family can expect regularly. And this is only for the smaller families. Furthermore, it is definitely not a continuation of regular family life, but an escape from it. In the large families, the oldest children are required, in some cases, to take care of the household each year while the parents go off for a few days of change. Many of the children have yearly short vacations at free camps, and this is a time of exhilaration and preparation for the family. Its climax comes when trains or buses loaded with the children of the neighborhood are "seen off" by parents, siblings, and other neighbors.

VI. FAMILY BUDGETING AND ALLOWANCES

Wherever there was a family council on budgeting and expenditures, it occurred in the middle-class family. In some cases the children are even given a vote on the purchasing of home improvements and new cars when something else has to be sacrificed for them. These children are pretty well aware of their fathers' salaries and what sort of arrangements are made between Father and Mother for household and personal expenses. Usually there is a set sum, given to the mother at whatever interval the father receives his pay. Children get allowances by the week, often supplementing them, in their teens, with money they earn, which is considered strictly their own.

The lower- and upper-class children know next to nothing about their parents' incomes or about budgeting. They are not called in to council on such subjects.

Most of the lower-class children do not get allowances, but simply ask for money, and are never sure whether or not they will get it. It came to light that the young married brother, or brother-in-law, is an especially good source to tap in this respect for these girls—in fact, older working siblings in the lower class showed considerable generosity toward all younger children. When these children are small and do odd jobs, the money they earn is their own. But when they grow older and have steadier work with better pay, they are supposed to contribute to the family in board.

All the upper-class children have their own allowances. When they were younger, this was the same sort of weekly sum that is still being meted out to the middle class at college age. By early teen age, however, the upper-class child's allowance is almost in every case in the form of a bank account, into which the father or mother deposits a check every month, ranging from $100 up. This is specified to be for certain purposes, and varies from "incidentals" to "all personal expenses and clothing, except fur coats." Some of the girls have private incomes, plus allowances, and some have full-time paying positions. But in all cases their incomes are considered their own, and there is no contribution to the family expected, except through personal gifts.

VII. PRESENT-GIVING

The middle class seems to enjoy gift-giving rituals and goes out of its way to provoke such occasions, quite apart from celebrations such as birthdays and Christmas. These rituals, as they have been described in an earlier chapter, are characteristic of this class. There are certain regulations concerning their gift-giving which may be added here, however. Gifts for non-holiday times may be food and necessities, but for birthdays and Christmas they are almost always extra luxuries. An exception is that of a needed dress for a special party; one that would not be forthcoming otherwise. Another exception is the gifts given to the middle-class father. From this report, he corresponds to the cartoonists' conception of him, in that he receives only the presents that he would have to buy for himself anyway: ties, shirts, socks, etc. An examination of upper-class gift-giving to Father leads to the possible explanation that the middle-class father is discriminated against chiefly because he indulges in so few hobbies, except smoking, that his wife and children are hard pressed to find interesting gifts for him.

The upper-class males do have hobbies which enable their families to give them wide varieties of presents. Golf, gunning, fishing, photography, stamp collecting, and so on, result in very different habits in family presentations. In this class, gift-giving is more restricted to appropriate occasions—birthdays, Christmas, and anniversaries predominating—and is on a more spectacular scale at these times. To give a downright necessity is something not to be tolerated. Even if such an article as a smoking jacket, underwear, or housecoat is given, it must be of the extraordinary sort that precludes its ever being bought by the recipient.

In the lower class, gift-giving is pretty well restricted to birthdays and Christmas. Even birthday celebrations belong chiefly to the smaller children. One girl interviewed responded matter-of-factly, "Oh, I didn't have any birthday this year. I was fifteen." A special dinner with ice cream and cakes is generally the only birthday festivity for parents and older children, except in the smallest families. Christmas is a more liberal time, but the gifts are predominantly in the form of foods of some kind. Another girl described Christmas at her house: a wooden bowl on the center of the dining-room table, containing presents for all the members of the family from the rest of the family. Every gift in the bowl is something to eat.

A very common ritual of the middle-class parent generation was the practice for family and close relatives to present a girl baby at birth, and on subsequent birthdays, with the kind of gift which was a symbol of what it was hoped her adult status would one day be. The most usual gift was a piece of sterling silver flatware, which gradually, through the years, was built up into a whole set. Jewelers aided in this conspiracy, keeping in their files the names of the recipient, the pattern of the silverware, and the pieces already accumulated. The gift second in popularity was the necklace to which a pearl was added annually. The initial gift was the largest, center pearl. Jewelers are still advertising their willingness to aid in this family ritual. In this way many a middle-class girl whose parents and friends might not have been able to present them all at once with these gifts at the proper time, were, upon marriage, equipped with two of the valued symbols of "gracious living."

VIII. HEIRLOOMS

Rituals that grow up around family heirlooms, or that feature the heirlooms prominently, are frequent, but present a very strong contrast in their relative popularity and absence in the different classes.

The upper class are the real collectors. They are either guarding a long family tradition, or are trying to establish one for future generations. Portraits, jewels, furniture, *objets d'art*, silverware, and even clothing are passed down, and each with a story attached to it. The articles and the stories sometimes become objects of public interest. Certain jewels, for instance, always appear at the first night of the opera season. Mrs. Edward Stotesbury's tiara is now famous in Philadelphia, and even its eccentricities of slipping to one side, and the technique used to keep it upright became public knowledge.[8]

At a less spectacular level, cherished pieces of jewelry and

[8] Ashley Halsey, Jr., "Ringmaster of the Social Circus," *Saturday Evening Post*, May 15, 1948, p. 36 ff.

furnishings are loaned for public exhibit. Clothing, chiefly christening robes and wedding dresses, are displayed at shows for charity purposes. A complete show of fashions, from Revolutionary times to the present, can be, and has often been, given by simply calling upon the upper class of the Philadelphia metropolitan area for the loan of their family heirlooms. The importance to individual families of having such possessions and of having traditions behind them is illustrated by a remark made by a woman whose home is full of them. When asked how she ever remembered the histories of all those heirlooms, she replied: "If you don't remember the story, you make one up. In two generations, it doesn't matter too much."

For a girl of the upper class to be married in her mother's or grandmother's wedding gown is most desirable, and is frequently done. A girl who was married in a gown described in the papers the following day as a T—— family gown, is still being guarded from the secret that the dress actually came from "the other side of the family" (the less socially important side), because the wearing of such a dress had been so very important to her.

The middle class also hands down jewelry, furniture, silverware, with stories connected, but they seldom come to public notice; there are fewer of them; and they are more in the nature of keepsakes and less of *objets d'art*. The family Bible, in which family records are kept, is an especially important heirloom in the middle class, even in cases where the records are the beginning of a tradition rather than a long-continued one. It is considered very significant to be married in a mother's wedding gown. But it is less often possible with girls of the middle class, because of quality, fashioning, and lack of good facilities for preserving them. Some article of family property, though, is usually found to represent the "old" part of the "something old, something new, something borrowed, and something blue" that is an important tradition of a middle-class wedding.

In the lower class, it seems almost as if there were no past, or as if what there was is best forgotten. What heirlooms were reported either spoke of former, better times in the family, or were a nostalgic remembrance of old-country days. There was a piano, a pair of candlesticks, and a fur coat that Mother had had when she was married and that had been handed down from daughter to daughter in successive stages of disrepair. To wear a mother's wedding dress is unthinkable. The dresses were actually long since gone and forgotten. But the girls, furthermore, seem to have no realization of the fact that their own mothers might at one time have been as young and attractive as they are now. This is in marked contrast to the attitudes of the girls of the other classes. One reason for this may be explained in the following family rituals.

IX. PICTORIAL REPRESENTATIONS OF THE FAMILY

A child can get his knowledge of his, and his family's past, only through symbolic representations. This may be in the form of written records, verbal communications (often connected with the aforementioned heirlooms), and pictorial representations. In the published autobiographies, the first two sources seemed of most importance. Naturally persons about to write their life stories for publication deliberately look up family records and approach other family members for anecdotes about ancestors. But with these writers, the telling of stories about the family in the past also constituted a significant part of early childhood family rituals. Many maiden aunts and grandparents lived in the homes with these children, and it was largely these relatives who were steeped in old family traditions and who thrilled the youngsters with repeated accounts of them. Even servants who had remained in the family for generations kept the family past alive, often through stories told to children at bedtime.

In the homes of the present-generation cases, there are few story-telling rituals, and those that occur do not deal with family history. Children do, of course, hear anecdotes about the family, but in no steady, regularized fashion. The only case of any such ritual was found in the home of an upper-class girl, and included three generations. In this family, all newspaper clippings publicizing activities of family members are collected and pasted into a scrapbook. To these are added programs from all events in which a member has participated: records of sports; scholastic, dramatic, and social honors won; announcements of graduations, fraternity memberships, christenings, engagements, weddings; and accounts of any honors won by family animals at shows. Each year, on New Year's Eve, before the guests arrive for the evening, but after the family is dressed in formal clothes, they all gather in the "trophy room" and sit around the fireplace to renew acquaintance with their past, assess the dying year's achievements, and tell family stories. This ritual was described as a challenge from the past to the future, to be invoked each year at a time when resolutions are at an inspirational high. People with rituals such as this do not find it difficult to picture Mother as a girl.

The method by which such an image is kept alive in the present-day families is, for the most part, through pictorial representations of the family, but such practices varied with the class.

The lower class, as represented here, is not a regular photograph-taking class. There are few pictures of the family members, except of the small babies, or of children at graduation. Photographs of members of past generations are almost non-existent. The children have no idea what the family looked like, or did, a generation or two ago.

But the upper class goes in for such pictorial recording at set times. In most of the families there is a stated interval, of about once a year or every other year, when the children are photographed. Furthermore, each large private social occasion or crisis rite in the family necessitates a picture to commemorate it. Ordinarily, photographers are called into the home for this purpose, where the family is pictured together and individually, in their own home setting amid their own belongings. In the so-called "horsey set," favorite family horses and dogs and cats are also included in some photographs. Many of the before-mentioned family heirlooms are prominently featured.

Preservation of pictures and portraits of earlier family members is common, and these are often valuable works of art. As such, they are a part of the actual home furnishings, and are not only acceptable to the children, but are objects of pride. Thus in this class there is not only a sense of family continuity and tradition, but the family lives, in the mind's eye, and for generations back.

In the middle class there are also set times for the photographing of the family. It is a less usual ritual, it is ordinarily a photographing of children alone, and there is a long gap between babyhood days and the day of graduation from grammar or high school. In these cases, the photographer is not often called into the home, but the subject sits in his studio. The resulting picture, then, does not include the home surroundings, or traditional possessions. The middle class also preserves pictures of former generations, but these are not exactly *objets d'art*, and usually if the photograph of Uncle Will, stiff and unattractive, is used as a piece of home furnishing, it is an abomination to the teen agers, who tolerate it because of Mother's sentiment toward it. These girls, many of them, can conceive of their family as a long line of young people growing up through the same succession of events which face them, but the pride in them is not so marked as it is in the upper classes. The evidences of their past are, rather, embarrassing, amusing, albeit endearing.

Summary

1. When the families under study are divided into social classes (lower, middle, and upper) according to ways of life that are acknowledged as different and labeled according to class stratification in the Philadelphia metropolitan area, it is found that their family rituals differ materially on a class basis. Rituals take their shape from the culture in which they arise, and different classes are different cultures.

2. The lower-class family, as represented in these cases, is one in which there is little connection with the past. The present is composed of individuals crowded into a space too small for comfort. Families are large. The religion is predominantly

Catholic. The economic situation is not one of affluence. Children see nothing in their families to stimulate the desire to perpetuate what they see. Opportunities for emotional satisfactions in the home are few, even for the adults. The rituals arising from these situations are, for the most part, rituals of expediency, to keep the home going, and to facilitate escape from home into a more exciting or promising outside world.

3. The middle class is more comfortably situated. There is enough physical space to permit of frequent family interaction, but not enough to allow much isolation of family members. Family finances are such that each member can hope to benefit by close coöperation. The past of the family is in their minds, but usually the present is better, and gives a challenge for the future. The family tone is one of hopefulness and optimism. There is a scorning, therefore, of habits that might lead in a downward direction, and a pressing forward toward a higher one, which tends to both moral and social carefulness. The rituals arising here show a coöperativeness of desire to reach these goals, as well as a genuine family "togetherness" in a home where there is need for it and the opportunity for it.

4. The upper class is guarding a way of life which is considered by them, and by many others, to be the desirable one. They have the time, for the most part the wealth, and the physical surroundings in which they can perpetuate it. The history of their family is intimately with them. It is something to conserve, and in which to take pride. Close association of the members is not so necessary within their set-up. Their way of life can be preserved by taking seriously the social symbols which are generally acknowledged as standing for it. Their rituals converge around these. They are more formalized than in the other classes, and they are more easily perpetuated from generation to generation because of the fortunate circumstances of their lives.

5. The rituals of the three classes, though arising from a way of life which springs originally from an economic foundation, are not, in these cases, differentiated purely on income bases. There are many middle-class families in the present study which

are the economic superiors of some of the upper-class families, while the incomes of some of the middle class closely correspond to some in the lower class. A way of life puts a family into association with others who have the same way, and in association these ways tend to be maintained. Expenditures are made on the basis of relative values and goals, the symbols of the respective classes being the values for which other things are sacrificed. Rituals result which derive from a class culture rather than from any one economic status group.

7

Family Ritual and the Family Cycle

I N THE EARLY part of this century, Rowntree described a regular economic cycle that occured in the life of the British working family. Its financial status went down with the arrival of several children and remained low until the children were of working age, at which time the family income increased and remained higher until the children left home. After this, at a late age, the family was again left in reduced circumstances.[1] Later studies have substantiated the concept of a family economic cycle and have suggested that it is not restricted only to the British working family. For sociologists these researches became significant not so much for the emphasis on family budget as for the deeper fact that lay behind them: that the family goes through successive stages of development as it progresses from youth to old age, and that this means successive changes in family relationships, needs, and activities. As Lawrence Frank puts it: "Families are always in transition, as the individual members of the family are growing, developing and maturing and aging, as they face the various tasks of life which confront them as individual men and

[1] B. S. Rowntree, *Poverty*, London, The Macmillan Company, Ltd., 1901.

women and boys and girls growing up, maturing, becoming members of our society. . . ."[2] Out of this social-dynamic point of view has come the classifying of the family cycle into certain stages: (1) the founding family; (2) the expanding family; (3) the contracting family. Frequently it is subdivided even further into (1) early marriage and the expectant family; (2) the beginning of child-bearing; (3) the pre-school family; (4) the family with teen agers; (5) the family as a launching center; and (6) the aging family.[3]

This latter classification of the family into six stages of development, called cyclical because they recur in the following generation, becomes something more than a convenient categorizing when inspected against the background of family rituals. Not only do the rituals vary in the same clear-cut stages, but the periods of changing from one stage to the next appear to be times of crisis and heightened emotions over the ritualistic procedures themselves. Sometimes the emotion is excitement and joy: at other times it is irritation or worse. But the change has to occur if the family is to mature normally. It is to these changes in family rituals, in relation to the family cycle, that this chapter is devoted.

I. EARLY MARRIAGE AND THE EXPECTANT FAMILY

Marriage is a time for a new deal in family ritual. It involves at least three different processes: (1) a conscious deliberation of each person to be married concerning certain rituals which must be abandoned and others which must be kept; (2) an adjustment of two separate ritual systems between the new husband and wife; and (3) the emergence of a new family ritual.

1. Case studies lead to the suggestion that one of the pleasurable anticipations of married life is the excuse it suddenly brings to slough off distasteful family procedures. This is the period at which interviewees have found it expedient to break

---

[2] Lawrence K. Frank, "Dynamics of Family Interaction," *Marriage and Family Living*, Vol. X, No. 3, Summer, 1948, p. 52.

[3] *Ibid.*

immediately with family customs that they felt had been too long endured out of respect for parents. With our cases, church-going and home religious rites often passed out of existence at this time. Mealtime ceremonials considered old fashioned and outmoded were exchanged for more simple procedures. This was the time to give up the weekly visit to Grandmother's and the gift-giving to distant relatives, under the excellent excuse of new impositions upon time and money. A sudden separation from parents during holidays, week-ends, and anniversary celebrations could be attempted simultaneously with the honeymoon, without seeming too cruel. All these changes have been confessed as deliberate plans, carefully considered before the wedding day. Some of the subjects, indeed, admitted that the spirit of sudden independence from the parental home which marriage gave to them resulted in their throwing overboard a good many rituals which, as time passed, they discovered were not quite so repressive after all, and which gradually crept back into their new homes. But at least a holiday from accustomed ritual was a common result of a marriage and the new deal in family life.

The freedom from the rituals, however, was not an unmitigated blessing in all cases, particularly when the young couple still lived within visiting distance of the parents. One parent who expressed herself on the changes that occurred when her eldest daughter married may represent here the feelings of others. This parent was a loving and conscientious mother. She had treasured family keepsakes to hand down to her children. All the holiday customs and other little rituals pleasurable to her family had been consciously perpetuated from the time of the birth of her first baby to the day of the children's departure from the fold. The home was rich in such celebrations, and because these meant hard work for someone she carried that burden, offering only the fun to the children. Even the neighbors' youngsters loved to gather in that home to share the ceremonies that their own mothers would not be bothered with. When the eldest daughter married, she who had always boasted about her family activities determined that she was not going to be the tied-down hausfrau that her mother had always been, nor was she going to have her modern apartment cluttered up with relics from the past. When her mother described this daughter's streamlined existence, she sighed with ill-concealed regret, "Ah well! Times change. And our children have to make their own lives." Many such parents originate rituals purposely and perpetuate them with some labor with the thought only of the rich heritage they are for their children. Some of those, in these case studies, who saw them sloughed off so unceremoniously were not so philosophical as this mother.

2. New husbands and wives thus came to marriage with carefully considered opinions of which rituals they wished to keep and which they wished to forget. All came with some rituals which were parts of life so unconsciously acted out that to live without them would be hardly like living. But the fact was that they both came, with their own ideas and experiences, to found one family. One of our cases frankly describes a situation which arose in her new home.

In my family (of seven members), we could hardly wait to get home from school and work to tell each other what we had all been doing during the day. We could not do this at dinner, because the maid was constantly coming in and out. So, every evening, ever since we had been small children, we all moved to the living room right after dinner and "let ourselves out." As we grew up, we took to having our coffee in the living room instead of at the table. This got us to the best part of the day more quickly and it was more intimate and impressive. . . . Then I got married. One of my wedding gifts from the family was a silver service with a tray large enough to accommodate coffee cups and saucers also. This thoughtful gift was one of my favorites because I could see just John and me sitting over our coffee in our new living room every evening, after we had been apart all day, swapping the day's events. It did not work out that way. John wanted his coffee during dinner. As soon as he got to the living room he picked up a newspaper or book and was completely silent for the rest of the evening. When I tried to talk he was irritated, and I never could talk until week ends, when we did catch up with each other. But the whole week between was like a chasm to me, and though during the daytimes I still thought of the day's happenings in terms of something to report to John that night, the evenings were horrible. I never had a chance to "let myself out"

nor to learn anything about John—but he never wanted me to leave
the room, just to sit there quietly. One evening, when I was full of
an incident that had occurred, John put down his book just long
enough to say: "Will you please shut up and let me get some rest!"
I went to my married sister to tell her that John and I could never
make a go of it. She explained to me that a man like John, who
teaches all day long, may very justifiably look forward to an evening
of completely silent, restful companionship. That had never occurred
to me. I had thought there was something deliberately sadistic about
somebody who did not do things the way we always did. I didn't
insist on my ritual after that, but I have to admit that I often feel
very much frustrated holding my speeches over until the weekend.

The effects of such situations upon individual marriages will
be discussed at length in a later chapter. It is therefore sufficient to indicate here that the first stage of the family cycle is
one in which two ritual systems and two sets of attitudes toward
them must be blended, must exist side by side, or one be domi-
nated by the other.

Two other facts are characteristic of this stage. The adjustment is somewhat simplified by having to deal only with adult-
type rituals, and involves for the most part only family pride
and personal idiosyncrasies. There are as yet no children to
exaggerate the importance of old family forms. The adjustment, however, is complicated by the fact that as long as there
are no children, considerable pressure is often brought to bear
on the young couple from both sides of the family. It has been
suggested in interviews during this study, though it would
certainly bear further investigation, that many parents do not
cut apron strings until they see their children in the role of
parents themselves. They may be married, but they are still
"free" to come home and to share all the accustomed family
celebrations. Further, they are not considered quite grown up
until they attain parenthood, and therefore still require a deal
of parental advice, even in respect to the ways in which they
conduct themselves in their new-founded homes. For the young
couple themselves, there is an extra weight of guilt about
breaking off the family customs, even to please their mates,
which cannot be rationalized by the thought of their prime

responsibility to their own children. In families that remain childless, the type of ritual to which they adjust remains at the adult level. Pressure from both in-laws also continues frequently to be a great source of difficulty until physical separation and/or psychological maturity weakens it. Specific rituals which have caused most conflict in this respect were holiday, Sunday, and religious observances, vacation rites, mealtime and entertaining ceremonies, and visiting kinfolk.

3. Obviously, out of the individual sifting and the mutual adjusting there grows a new ritual system. Couples devise their own rites consciously, in the excitement of their new freedom, surroundings, and belongings, and find others forming inevitably in the daily process of living together. A girl commented upon the slovenly way in which meals were served in her home —from stove to table. She was engaged to be married, and she had kept a scrapbook of highly colored pictures from women's magazines in which small tables were decorated with flowers, candles, and pretty pottery dishes. She was interested in recipes for aspics and fluffy desserts. This is what she was going to have in her home when her husband came home tired from work. This, of course, is the youthful enthusiasm of anticipation—the stuff of which dreams are made. Nevertheless it is the stuff of which many changes were made in the homes of new-married subjects. Young couples who moved from large formalized homes into tiny apartments, who broke off their friendships with childhood chums to mix with business associates, originated very distinct formal procedures of their own —as did those who left behind them homes whose traces would embarrass the young couple in their new surroundings. It was the forming of such "foreign" systems, as well as the dropping of old ones, that frequently caused raised eyebrows and harsh words from watching parents, younger siblings, and past friends.

The building up of a new ritual system for a newly married pair was seen to be not only a time of decision, adjustment, and creation, but one of criticism from, and defensiveness toward, outsiders.

II. THE BEGINNING OF CHILD BEARING

With the knowledge that the erstwhile bride and groom are to become parents, our cases show a change, first in their attitude toward family ritual, and second in certain of the rites.

We eliminate at the outset those few cases in which the knowledge was anything but a pleasure and in which adult rituals were maintained to the complete exclusion of the child even after it had arrived. This sort of situation is a research project in itself, and cannot be discussed fruitfully on the basis of our present material.

In all other cases, not only a feeling of superficial pride, but a very deep sense of a changing role and status of the family occurred. Though at the time it was not consciously thought out in these terms, ritual took on a new meaning. It was no longer just a repressive procedure to be freed from, or a practice to promote pleasure and to cement relationships between married lovers; but it was the means through which the heritage from the past was to be handed down to the future. In other words, parents-to-be were adopting the same attitudes toward family ritual that they had so recently resented in their own parents. This changed significance led to the following results in our cases.

1. With the beginning of child-bearing, religious rituals, holiday customs, and kinship celebrations came into interest for redefining and, where mates did not agree, caused new difficulty. It is one thing to quit or modify such rituals out of sheer laziness or to keep peace with a mate. This can be rationalized as the privilege of maturity or as unselfishness. It is quite another thing, however, when a child arrives. A wholly different orientation leads new parents to consider rituals appropriate not just to themselves but to the coming generation. Newlyweds who became parents soon after their marriage were the ones for whom these rituals became a point of greatest tension when the first child arrived. They had hardly had time to adapt to each other's rites at an adult level when a new emotional disturbance concerning them occurred. Though

these cases were in the minority in our study, it is suggested here that this may be a general problem in married life, if our cases are characteristic. For Paul Glick has stated that "Following marriage, about a year elapses before the average mother bears a child. This interval has not varied greatly since 1917."[4] In families in which there was a period of adjustment of three years or more before a child arrived, there seemed to be a willingness and an established technique for ritual readjustment which led to more satisfactory results during this period. Even in a few cases of very late marriage, where it might be assumed that rigid patterns of adult behavior might change with difficulty, the arrival of children did not cause husband-wife conflict over ritual as it did in the case of the youthful marriages immediately disturbed by child-bearing.

2. For the most part, with the actual birth of the first baby, ritualistic roles developed in the process of constructing entirely new procedures. There came the very set establishment of a division of labor concerning the child. Mother and Father had definite duties as to feeding, changing, and bathing. Practices of Father's taking over to give Mother some recreation were instituted. Definite times for Father's playtime with baby were established. Baby himself was described in case after case as being the originator of a specific family ritual: choosing a certain time after one feeding, when both parents were present, to be on his most charming behavior. When this was admired, played up to and repeated, there came to be the dependable hour during which Baby would smile seductively, gurgle and coo; and the parents, responding by certain definite forms of play as encouragement, were knit close together with Baby in mutual family admiration. In cases where there was no serious ritual maladjustment at marriage, the child-bearing period was one in which new family rites of this sort were many, exciting, and rich in content and emotional satisfaction. None of these could endure for long, but the impressive feature of these rites is that they tended to recur with the birth

[4] Paul Glick, "The Family Cycle," *American Sociological Review*, Vol. 12, No. 2, April, 1947, p. 167.

of each new baby, and in the same form. They therefore became the way to behave when a new child arrived. Even more important, older children became accustomed to these forms as they were repeated, and assumed them to be the right ways, the proper definition of roles, when they formed their own families.

3. A number of families of upper and middle class instituted a very formal ritual with the birth of the first baby, as a symbol of the father's pride and his appreciation to his wife. In the upper class, a gift to the mother from the father, and usually jewels, became a custom which was repeated as each new child arrived. In two of these families, the flowers sent by the young husband to the hospital were the beginning of a standing weekly order of flowers for Mother, which have arrived dependably ever since. With the middle-class families, a personal gift or some household equipment was given. In one family with five children, the modern gas range, the electric refrigerator, the washing machine, the electric mangle, and the deep-freezer were coincident with the arrival of each of the five children. No doubt those five are hoping for a new baby soon—and a television set.

4. In spite of the enduring of comic cartoons concerning the interference of grandparents, our cases concluded that becoming parents had actually lessened the tensions between couples and their own parents as far as those tensions involved family rituals. This may be attributable to several things. (a) The new parents became noticeably more orthodox in their views with the advent of children and tended more toward the traditional, which pleased their families. (b) It became a point of pride for new parents to reënter kinfolk celebrations to show off the new baby. (c) A common interest arose between grandparents and parents which offset antagonistic ones, and led to rituals commonly shared with pleasure.

III. THE PRE-SCHOOL FAMILY

The pre-school family period was the period richest in the formation of many trial-and-error procedures which crystallized into set forms. At this time the two-generation family is learning to live together. Parents and children, siblings and new siblings, are working out a pattern of family life. No one has much firsthand experience, and successful procedures, discovered quite accidentally after many false starts, become set. (a) Disciplinary rituals arose in this way, and children were ever thereafter subjected to forms which seemed most successful at that time. (b) The pre-school period is the time during which the mother and the children are most frequently together. The rites enjoyed at this time were, by a very large majority, mother-determined rituals. (c) As has already been suggested in chapter 4, the children themselves are apt to be rigid ritualists at this age. Arnold Gesell has noted that two-and-a-half-year-olds are themselves insistent upon regularity of procedures. Deviations are upsetting, and children are very vocal about them. The way in which one such ritual arose is characteristic of the case-study family rites at this level:

When David came home from the office, he liked to romp with the children after dinner. It was the only chance he had all day to see them. This privilege could not be denied, but it excited the children before bedtime and created a family crisis every night. David got tired and wanted to hear the news; the children were peevish and noisy and did not want to go to bed; and I (their mother) was at my wits' end to keep family peace. One night, I decided to read to the children if they got into bed quickly. The next night they asked if I would read a story if they would get to bed quickly. From that time on, until the last baby went to school, there was no question about what happened in our house at bedtime. The children had their romp with David; they were eager to go upstairs afterward; David heard his news broadcast in peace and quiet before I got downstairs again; and the every-evening quarrel was ironed out to everyone's satisfaction. But from a simple experiment in reading one night, we ended up with a ritual, a full-fledged ritual with a time and a place, a determined type of reading material, and with many little observances and rules and regulations that we collected as time went on.

Ordinarily, a smooth household regimen is most important at the pre-school family stage. The family is not at a high economic peak and the home is crowded; the mother, at the busiest time of her life, has need for order; small children require it for security. When such a regimen as the above turns into ritual loved for itself and not just for its expediency, it serves a double purpose. In just this way the families under study have developed many such rites at this period, which, starting out as trial-and-error attempts at expediency, have turned into something much more rich and lasting.

IV. THE FAMILY WITH TEEN AGERS

A division which makes a jump from the pre-school family to the family with teen agers seems an arbitrary one, and one too wide for adequate description of the family cycle. However, as far as family ritual is concerned, our cases suggest no need for an added category here. Actually, pre-school rituals, until teen age time when noticeable variations arise, seem to crystallize and endure. Discipline, holiday, birthday, recreation, and household procedures are established early and remain much the same. With the advent of school days, new procedures surrounding bedtime and arising (see chapter 6, on Family Rituals and Class Differentials), the doing of homework and the entertaining of playmates do appear, but, for the most part, this period is one of separation from family which does not lead to the stimulation of new family rituals. The well-known "latency period" seems also to be a period of latency in family ritual. With the coming of teen age, however, although this is described as a time of increased emancipation from the family, there appears a new era of family ritual development, and probably for at least three reasons. (a) Children are nearing adulthood. In interests, activities, and abilities they begin to approach their parents on an equal basis, and a new congeniality-relationship is in order. (b) Parents feel the imminent danger of separation if companionship or domination is not well established. (c) Our culture stresses "watching" and "keeping in touch" with children at this crucial time when interest in the opposite sex brings new dangers. According to our cases, this is what occurs:

1. It is now that rites stressing maturity and responsibility

appear. The upper-class girl makes her debut. The Jewish boy is feted through the Bar Mizvah. Boys and girls receive a front-door key and a driver's license—all at a definite age. These are the modern equivalents of the times mentioned in published autobiographies when boys got their first long trousers and girls put on long dresses, put up their hair and were allowed their first high-heeled shoes. Dating starts, and gives rise to new family rites. One girl explains her own:

Saturday and Sunday nights were "Date nights." We were expected to accept invitations. One felt as if one degraded the family a bit by staying at home, alone on those nights. But, if someone "just impossible" should call, we could always say politely, "I'm sorry, but I have an engagement." This engagement was a standing one— with Mother. And even if Charles Boyer should have 'phoned subsequently, that date with Mother could not have been broken. This stringency was not a penalty for saying no to an eligible male, but due to our immediate family tradition that we never turned down one invitation and then accepted a better one for the same time. . . . Upon returning home from a date, my sister and I always went first into Mother's bedroom where she was unfailingly awake, and reported the hour, which she already knew precisely, and told her whether or not we had had a good time.

2. Rites tend to become sex-divided in our families at the teen-age period. Formerly Mother was the presiding elder, and Father fitted into his space as allotted by her. Now Mother and the girls, and Father and his sons suddenly find much in common, and apart from the other family members of the opposite sex. Saturday is still family day, but it frequently becomes a day of shopping or parties for the ladies, and of fishing or other sports activities for the gentlemen. Rituals of household regimen are readjusted, so that big boys are relieved of humiliating female chores. Even vacation rituals are frequently changed at this time into two separate vacations—one for the women and one for the men. Many little informal but set rituals of a purely personal and almost inverted-status nature arise. For example, one boy described the ritual that grew up then and still exists.

When I was a kid, I used to borrow my father's ties once in a while, and felt very grown up wearing them. But now that I work after school, and go out on dates, I have more new ties than he does. So we have a little family custom that makes everyone laugh. Every time I get a new tie, I take my oldest, most shot one, off my tie rack and put it on Dad's. He always notices my new one—so he looks for the one I left for him. Then, next morning, he puts it on and comes down to breakfast with his chest all swelled out: "See my 'new' tie?" And all the family roars.

3. In a number of cases, families which have been too harried to stress rites of formal etiquette suddenly realize this responsibility at the age of intensified social relationships. One parent, who decided it was high time that her children learned to eat dinner in the dining room as she had always done in her own home, and launched such a formalized ritual without notice, was attacked by considerable guilt-feeling when her oldest exclaimed with awe: "Are we going to eat in the *dining room*—and with *candles!*" They never thereafter had an evening meal in the breakfast nook. This sort of formalized etiquette ritual enters the picture at just this period for a number of the families in which parents are foreign-born. In these cases, it is a child, usually a daughter, who attempts to institute it, often successfully but after some conflict. These cases have suggested the possible correlation of presence of daughters and assimilation in this sort of family. It seems from the cases that in such a home girls are more easily able to introduce forms which make a home acceptable for the entertaining of American-born friends, and that a family of boys is at a distinct advantage in this respect.

4. At just this teen-age period, with the beginning of near-adult social life, and the cultural emphasis on dangers for youth, a class separation in family rituals is noticeable. In the upper-upper class, parents and children begin to share family rituals, often for the first time. Before this period, the parents' life is social: the children's under the direction of nurses, governesses, teachers, maids, etc. But now, suddenly, children begin to share the interests of their parents. All sorts of family procedures

grow up. Children now always come to table with parents, and are included in sports activities, play bridge with the family on certain evenings, enter into regularized guest-entertainment and regular social events outside the home. Their rituals come to be on a near-equality basis. In the middle-class home, it is more like a pretended equality basis. The spirit is one of deliberately creating confidence in order to keep in touch with the children. The family council, the evening snack, the doing of dishes as a ruse for daily family reporting, the post-date conference, are all procedures which are devised to create moments of family intimacy in which to foster child frankness and confidence.

V. THE FAMILY AS A LAUNCHING CENTER

Gradually, in the ideal American family, children win both adult equality with parents and independence, even though they remain under the same roof. That this ideal is not often attained is well established in our case records as far as family ritual is concerned, for the period during which children are grown, but still dependent, is one of extreme tension over rituals. Even those adults in the study who now look back with pride to their family rituals, admit that, during the launching period, many of them were procedures submitted to only out of cowardice. This is the time when many of the cases decided to dispense with family rituals when they married—only to take them up again when their own children arrived. A doctoral thesis now in preparation suggests that one part of parent-child conflict at the college level stems from the fact that parents expect children who are themselves overburdened with career preparation to give as much time as ever to family rituals of all sorts.[5] This is borne out in the present study. Furthermore, when the launching period was toward marriage rather than a career, most daughters became equally restive under, and hypercritical of, family forms; though a few of them in very well adjusted homes took over the mother role, under

[5] Margaret Scoon Wilson, "Relations of College Girls With Their Parents," University of Pennsylvania Thesis, in manuscript.

maternal supervision, as a deliberate preparation. As for the boys, at this period, a lack of conflict over, or lack of complete separation from, the usual family rites seemed almost pathological.

There was one outstanding exception in our case studies to the negative influences of family rituals at the launching center stage. This is in cases where children are earning their own money and have a high degree of independence-feeling. In these cases, there is the development of rituals which have the purpose of repaying the parent, usually Mother, of presenting gifts at specific times, of entertaining her on certain days, or of taking over the household to free her once a week.

VI. THE AGING FAMILY

In the cases included in this study, the aging family meant for the most part the one from which the children had departed for establishments of their own. The cases are few. But since this stage of the family is becoming increasingly significant in our population and gets scant attention, any observations from actual case records may be of value.

Suggestions from the present analysis are that aging people may fall into ritualistic patterns as naturally and rigidly as do two-and-a-half-year-olds. They like regularity and security, and they need stimulus and interests. Furthermore, since the aging family (defined as the one from which children have departed) is not actually so old as it used to be, this is a critical time in respect to personal problems and family organization; and a time at which ritual can be of great value in maintaining companionship and extra-occupational interest, after children have homes of their own.

Our few cases suggest three things: (a) This is the time when there is an opportunity for parents to return to the "selfish" rituals enjoyed in early married days before the children arrived with their demands; and these rites can be a great source of satisfaction. This was one course adopted successfully. (b) Another was for the parent family to remain the center of holiday rites for all married children, and this resulted in unequal success. (c) Most striking of all was the success of rituals of all kinds innovated between grandparents and grandchildren. More than 50 per cent of the case recorders reported early childhood rituals at their grandparents' homes as being completely satisfying and looked back upon with nostalgia. In respect to intra-generational relationships, this was interesting enough to give pause.

VII. THE FAMILY CYCLE AS A CONCEPTUAL TOOL

The concept of the family cycle is, like all other conceptual tools, a useful and meaningful device which nevertheless has its limitations. Families do not always develop through these six stages, nor at times fit into any one of them.

1. Obviously, the childless family reaches the first stage only and develops its changing relationships and needs and rituals on an entirely different basis. Even when it ages, it does not fit into the defined classification of the aging family. This situation would make an interesting study in itself.

2. Even more important from the point of view of the developing family and its ritual is the fact that children are not all born at once, do not reach teen age, or become launched all at the same time. In large families, all stages are often represented at the same time. Even in the small modern families within this study, age spans are great in certain cases. In one, there are three children, all girls. When the oldest was sixteen, and the second one seven, a new baby arrived. What this may mean to family rituals can be best illustrated by the despairing remarks of a mother of four, separated only by eleven years.

After dinner, I am supposed to read to Tim, aged five. Althea, the ten-year-old, needs me to put her hair in curlers, sit on her bed and recast the day. Anne and Bill, fifteen and sixteen, want me all dressed up to receive their dates "properly." Their father would also like to see me once in a while in the evening, prepared for intelligent reading and entertaining. Now how on earth can I set up a good system for all of these people at the same time?

3. Some of our families were formed when the parents-to-be were middle aged. This is not "cricket" so far as the concept

of the family cycle is concerned. But it is happening more frequently than formerly that this sort of marriage produces children. In one case, the husband who had had children in a former marriage by a very austere wife, started at fifty to raise a new little family. He plunged into the ritualistic endowing of family life with the fervor of a twenty-year-old, as an obvious compensation for something he had missed. On the other hand, another couple of middle age who loved their child were utterly incapable of devising any but adult rituals when their child arrived, or to fit in with his little attempts to form some for them.

4. Another deviation from the pure concept, as found in our study, was the make-up of the aging family. For the most part, the children had left home. But there were also these cases: homes in which unmarried adults of the spinster and bachelor type are living at home; and homes in which married children, with and without their spouses and offspring, are still living with their parents. Family ritual, in such instances as all those cited above, cannot be related very meaningfully to any of the designated stages in the family cycle, and yet are of some significance in themselves, since they may be quite general.

Summary

1. When analyzed according to the family cycle, the cases under study reveal that the change from one stage of the cycle to another is often a time of increased tension in family life in respect to family rituals. It is noticeable that many parents find it difficult to relinquish the last stage; and the degree of tension seems largely dependent upon parental attitudes of possessiveness or freedom, in letting children take the natural next step in the direction of growing up and away.

2. It also seems marked that families differ in their success in ritualized relationships at different stages of the cycle. Some parents are extraordinarily clumsy in instituting satisfactory rites for small children, yet become adept at the teen-age level. Exactly the reverse is true in other families.

3. Many families, in their description, do not conform at all to any stage described in the family cycle. Some of them go through three stages at one time. Others are completely unclassifiable by these categories, but are just as significant in themselves, and therefore suggest the addition of new categories for study.

4. These deviations being admitted, certain generalizations concerning family rituals in relation to the family cycle may be stated from the cases here presented:

(a) Early Marriage and the Expectant Family. Here, rituals at an adult level have to be adjusted between the partners who always have some differences in ritual background. They may be assimilated, exist side by side, or one may dominate over the other.

(b) The Beginning of Child-bearing. This is a period during which family ritual takes on a new meaning. Since adolescent days, the husband and wife have been tending away from traditional family procedures. They now come to have meaning, traditionally, as a heritage to the future, and are frequently reëstablished exactly at this time.

(c) The Pre-School Family. This period is rich in the innovation of the most elementary rituals of child-rearing and household regimen. The process is very largely trial-and-error, but once culminating in a rite, the rite is strongly supported by both parent and child and is apt to endure exactly until teen-age time.

(d) The Family with Teen Agers. Ritual, at this stage, seems to multiply and to have new function: to prepare children for adult socialization; to prevent them from complete separation from the family; and to guard them through a dangerous biological change.

(e) The Family as a Launching Center. This part of the cycle seems the most tension-creating and disruptive of family rituals. Parents over-eagerly try to perpetuate rituals, and children over-zealously try to be free of them. The results are that ritualistic situations are strained, and that children often quit ones which they later redefine and readopt.

(f) The Aging Family. In cases where the aging family is defined as the parent couple left alone, family ritual becomes important because: (1) older people are physically and psychologically disposed to such regimen; (2) there is an opportunity to return to loved rituals that enriched married life before children arrived; and (3) grandparent-grandchild rituals seem to be especially satisfying to both generations. Since, however, the aging family is becoming younger, there are many variations of this stage of the cycle which are worthy of further study.

8

Three Generations of Family Ritual

HE KINDS of rituals described up to this point fall into two classes: those which have been born out of the experiences of an immediate family group, and those which have been handed down from past generations. Both kinds, however, have been described for the most part as they happened to exist at a moment in family life. Important to an understanding of these rituals is the discovery of *how* they spring up and *why* they are handed down or discarded. This process can be discovered only by following family rituals over a period of generations. This would show what really happens when two people, each with his own family ritual, marry; what they preserve for their children; whose rituals survive; how they are coördinated and modified; and how new children in a new generation affect old rituals and give rise to different ones. In a word, the processes of family ritual innovation, continuity, and discontinuity can be traced only in a record which follows the same family for many years. For this purpose, the present chapter consists of a three-generation study of family ritual.

· 154 ·

Selection of Family

The Adams family was selected for certain reasons. First, it was observed as a family that *has* rituals. These rituals are of a very visible sort, obvious to anyone who even casually enters into the home. It was not known, however, whether these structures were built up during the present generation or if they were of a traditional nature. Second, it was known that this family study would not be complicated by racial, nativity-class, or religious conflicts in their rituals. All elements of the family entering into this story are of old American Protestant stock of many generations. Third, the family represents the middle way in American life, both socially and economically. It does not place at extremes in either scale. Fourth, the adult family members of two generations are people constantly available, are interested and coöperative people, and all with the training and intelligence to understand the meaning and aims of such a study. After years of some experience in interviewing and case recording, the authors chose these people as being excellent subjects in so far as intellectual honesty and lack of inhibitions in talking about family matters are concerned. Fifth, the children of the third generation, too young to do much speaking for themselves on this particular subject, have been almost continuously observable in their actual family setting, from the birth of the youngest up to the present time— a period during which a *new* family, with its rituals, was actually formed. Sixth, the time span represented, from before the turn of the century to the present day, covers the period of greatest and most rapid social change—the first generation appearing at the beginning of its onset; the second, after World War I; and the third, at the close of World War II.

Limitations of Study

Limitations are apparent. (1) To cover all rituals in a family history is very difficult. It is the authors' experience that people questioned speak of current ones, and then the most obvious ones of an earlier family period. In the present investigation it has been relatively easy to cover the current rituals and to trace them back with specific directioning. This, of course, emphasizes continuities and innovations. Coverage is the more difficult, however, the farther back in time the investigation extends. People forget details of rituals of fifty or more years ago even when questioned about them specifically. It goes without saying that they do not spontaneously recall a number of rituals which did exist, but have passed out of existence. This means that discontinuities do not show up so frequently as survivals. The authors have attempted to remedy this by presenting, via questionnaire, lists of rituals in earlier American family life as found in autobiographies of that era, but they cannot hope to have found a complete remedy. (2) The three generations of the Adams family live together in one house, which is divided into two apartments. Within them, the grandparent generation and the parent-and-child generation live in physical separation as two family units. This adds a factor to their situation which may further increase *actual* continuity. It has, on the other hand, greatly facilitated the observation of changes which have occurred during the four years since this "separation"—which came with the marriage of the second generation. (3) No family is typical—even of the native-stock Protestant American family. This history is described not so much to show *which* rituals survive and decline in a family, as to try to discover some principles which have led to ritual survival, consolidation, decay, innovation. It cannot pretend even to answer all questions about such processes generally. The authors believe, however, that certain principles are suggested in the unfolding of this story which may be valid for more general projection, and which, it is hoped, seem plausible enough to lead to more investigation of the same sort, for purposes of verification or disproof. (4) A detailed description of all rituals which can be found in a three-generation study would form a book in itself. Since our material must be confined to a chapter, those rituals have been selected for description which have figured prominently in other case records already described and which are, therefore, familiar to the reader. Though this means that the story is not complete as it was gathered, it may tend toward greater emphasis on process and less distraction from it through introduction of new types of rituals.

The Family Study

The Adams family rituals will be described in their own words: exactly as written by them in the first months of the study, and as nearly as possible verbatim, from later interviews. For purposes of analysis and comparisons, their story will be presented in the following steps: (1) a brief sketch of family background of each generation: (2) accounts of selected rituals as described by each adult member of the family in his own generation, and in order of generation, with observations of the authors bracketed in the context and a brief comment concluding each separate type of ritual; (3) interpretations of the Adams family ritual process; and (4) the authors' summary.

I. FAMILY BACKGROUND

A. Mr. Adams was born in Iowa, on a farm, from which he moved to the closest town, into a ten-room house, when he was three years old. When he was twelve, the family moved to a seven-room home, after a fire had burned out the entire business district of their town. His father and mother lived there for the rest of their lives. There were two older sisters. Mr. Adams writes:

My mother had been a teacher before she married, but after marriage her time was completely filled with housekeeping and club work. Father was a farmer, merchant (meat markets a specialty), law consultant, and politician. Later in life he took up the business of tiling. He owned a large mole ditcher which pulled the tile into the ground in order to drain swamp ground. Politics claimed his interest mainly during middle life, and although he was content with small offices, such as that of sheriff, marshal, etc., he was one of the "powers behind the throne" and quite influential in State politics.

B. Mrs. Adams was born in Missouri, where she spent most of her childhood with her parents and a younger brother, in a twelve-room home. The father had been born in this house, and both children were also. Mrs. Adams' mother is specified as "homemaker," and her father as a physician specializing in cancer. She writes: "He was one of an unbroken line of doctors, the youngest of whom is my brother's son, now in medical school."

These two married and had one child, a daughter.

C. Janet was born in Key West, Florida, spending most of her life in Tennessee and Philadelphia, but moving very frequently. She says:

> The longest we ever lived in one house was eight years. That house had eleven rooms and was about the size we usually rented. It, and one other, which was a duplicate of the one we finally bought and now occupy, are the ones that stand out most in my mind.

Her mother was a social worker and teacher—at present with the public school system—and her father was a concert pianist, teacher, and composer of music.

D. Tom, Janet's husband, was born and spent his childhood in Baltimore, Maryland, in a twelve-room house. His mother was a housewife and his father an engineer and lawyer (engineering law). When Tom was six his father died, and his mother remarried. He had had three sisters. With the remarriage he acquired two step-brothers, and eventually one half-brother. Up to the time his father died, a great-aunt and a paternal grandmother and grandfather also lived with the family.

Janet and Tom have two children, a boy and a girl aged three and four, respectively.

E. The children, Catharine and Tommy, live in West Philadelphia, Pa. The house in which they live with parents and grandparents consists of two separate apartments, one of which accommodates them with their mother and father, and the other, Mr. and Mrs. Adams. Their mother is a lecturer in Comparative Religion, but says: "The preferred emphasis is on 'housewife';" and their father is a civil engineer.

All of the adults contributing to the study were college-educated: the men included (and their predecessors for many generations back) were at some time engaged in professional cr semi-professional work, and the women were housewives and/or of professional status also. The adult contributors are still working at their professions. They are all accustomed to living in moderately large homes and to considerable permanence of residence during childhood, with the exception of Janet, whose moves were frequent but for whom housing conditions remained fairly stable.

II. THE FAMILY RITUALS

A. *Mealtime:*

MR. ADAMS:

Did we eat at certain hours? Definitely. Breakfast was always at seven sharp, very sharp, for any time later was considered so close to dinner as to spoil both meals. Dinner was at high noon, but owing to the stubbornness of school authorities in insisting upon certain hours for dismissal there had to be some flexibility here. Supper was at six and while a trifle less sharp than breakfast, it ran it a close second. As I was on a more or less restricted diet during my earlier years, I had supper between four and five o'clock with "the woman" and I was snug in bed by the time the family assembled.

The family always ate together in the dining room. Everyone had a place at the family table, including the "hired girl." As a part of her duties included waiting on the table, she was here and there a great deal of the time.

Father did what carving was necessary and served the meats. The vegetables and fruits were put on the table in bowls and passed. Mother had, as did practically all housekeepers of the time, a service of everyday dishes and hardware, but she also had fine china and silverware for company.

When there was company, and there frequently was, the "hired girl" served the dinner and ate in the kitchen. We children were allowed to have guests at meals provided permission had been granted ahead of time.

The conversation at family meals consisted of lively political or club discussions between mother and father, generally, but the children were not cut out of the conversation. Questions were often asked concerning school work or general doings, but we did not volunteer such information unless it was requested.

Our mealtime rites were a winter-summer hook-up with little if any variation according to season.

MRS. ADAMS:

We ate at set hours: approximately 7:30, 12:30, and 6. Father sat at one end, Mother at the other; Brother on one side; I on the other. The whole family ate together, and in the dining room. There was special china, silver, and glassware for large dinner parties. Otherwise the same service was used all the time. Guests were invited to meals at any time. The help did the work of mealtimes. On special occasions or as a treat for the family, Mother would prepare some dish that she did exceptionally well—the favorite was biscuit. When I grew older, I usually made a cake for celebration days, such as birthdays. Father did the carving at the table. Mother served the desserts that were not prepared in separate portions.

Conversation was on the topic of mutual interest at the moment.

The only changes in mealtime customs were those of seasonal foods, except that in the very warm weather we frequently permitted the help to prepare salads, pressed meats, cold breads, desserts, etc., and leave the kitchen after the noon meal. On those days, Mother and I put the evening meal on the table.

There were no before-bed snacks, unless my father was detained by his work. In that case, it was always I who gave him something to eat when he came home. Then, he and I talked about the patients' illness, conditions, treatments, etc.

JANET:

Our meals were more or less regular with some deviations due to Dad's teaching schedules: in general at 7:30, 12 or 1; and 6. Saturday and Sunday we ate when the mood to prepare a meal struck us unless Dad was playing a church organ. Even when Dad had an organ, our schedule was very flexible. Breakfast would be late. Dinner usually came in the middle of the day, Saturday lunch and Sunday supper were the most fun of any meals in the week, since they consisted of delicatessen stuff so dear to a child's heart and stomach. Also, they might be eaten anywhere, and in nice weather were sometimes taken to the park. The "best" Saturday lunches were sandwiches and tea (by means of a "Sterno" stove) in Dad's downtown studio.

Dad sat at the head of the table, Mother on one side, me on the other. When there was company, Mother moved to the foot of the table. The whole family ate together even if meals had to be way off schedule to wait for or accommodate one member. Meals were in the dining room, unless rushed, or Saturday lunch and supper and Sunday supper—then in the kitchen.

We had everyday plated silver, and heirloom solid silver, oh so formal, for state occasions or company. Birthdays, Christmas, etc., brought it out just for the family. The heirloom china is a complete service of Haviland, from pre-Civil War days. This china has been passed down since then to the eldest daughter of Mother's side of the family upon her marriage. It is now in my possession and will be given to Catherine when she marries. The flat silverware comes from both sides of the family. When I was married, Mother gave me her mother's silver, and she uses her father's family silver. Catherine will one day fall heir to the set I am using now.

All of us did the work. Both my parents can cook, and Dad is proud of a skill that he developed as a hobby, having started as necessity in his boyhood in the West, where men had to cook. We all worked together until the work was done. Dad did the carving at the table.

The day's events were usually recounted at table. Whoever had the most exciting tale to tell "got the floor" first. Any and every subject interested us, but most common were psychology, history, music, literature, and above all others, people. There was a great deal of training in "Family": names of members of every branch of progenitors, coats of arms, family history, and the historic great of the family. A heavy emphasis on family traditions, standards and behavior, and some discussion in a foreign language every day.

Summer schedules were always more lax. When Mother was out of school, even breakfast was later.

Dad always asked the blessing before the meal began.

Tom:

We did not eat at set hours, the family was too large. Only Mother and Father (or step-father) had special places, at the head and foot of the table. We ate in the dining room, but the whole family did not eat together except by chance. We had everyday and company dishes, silver and linens, and best for company, but no heirloom ones.

Mother and sisters did the work, and with the servants when there were some. Mother did the carving in the kitchen.

There was no certain kind of mealtime conversation, since Mother was entirely deaf and the family too large for a single conversation.

The regime was the same, summer and winter.

Whoever wanted a snack before bedtime went and got one.

Children (as reported by Janet):

We eat at 7:00, 12 or 1; and 6. On weekends and holidays there are no set times. All have our own places. At the small, square table, we sit: Tom at the head, I at the foot and babies between. But at the oval table, we sit alternately, parent and child, parent and child, around one side of the table. When guests come to meals, they range on the other side of the oval table. (The oval table is a family piece and is not used daily while the babies are still young and destructive.) We always eat in the dining room, and always together. From the time a baby is strong enough to sit up, it comes to the table. We use the heirloom service mentioned before for special occasions, and everyday service at other times. Everybody does the work. Even the babies like to play at helping and wipe their own plastic dishes. Tom does the carving at table. Our conversation is practically the same as it was in my own family. I always ask the blessing.

In summer, Tom's meal hours remain, but the children and I join my parents at their breakfast though we have eaten, and just talk. We often eat on the back porch, (dinner) in summer.

Comment

Mr. and Mrs. Adams' mealtime rituals had been very similar from childhood. Hours were set, but permitted of flexibility for the greater value of having all members present; each member had a special place at table; table service was similarly arranged in each case for family and for "special occasions;" and conversation was a lively family affair. There was little change in these aspects of the ritual when Mr. and Mrs. Adams made their own home together. The forms remained approximately the same, and Mrs. Adams was prepared for even greater flexibility to suit her husband's convenience because her own father had been a doctor, with uncertain hours of work. There were, however, noticeable changes. First, Mrs. Adams continued professional work after she became a wife and mother. This made weekends in that home a time for special relaxation of regular weekday procedures resulting in weekend mealtime rituals of a different and special nature. Second, Janet remained an only child, and the family was characterized by no sharp competition between child level and adult level. Their table seating was modified into an arrangement which would seat them all closer together. Table conversation was "of mutual interest" like Mrs. Adams', but was not divided into children's and adult's topics as was Mr. Adams'. It was a unit. Third, with Mother out of school, the summer schedule of greater laxity became a pleasure. A use of other places than the dining room for meals grew more popular at these times. Fourth, the best silver became even more significant as "heirloom" silver, having passed down one more generation, and at table there was a conscious, successful effort to perpetuate the memory of past family generations, their names, deeds, traditions, etc.

Tom's mealtime rites had been quite different. But he married into a "going concern." The Adams' rituals prevailed, and Tom adopted the hours, all-family participation, taking over the traditional task of father's carving at the table. But certain changes resulted. Janet asks the blessings, although it had been traditional in her family for the father to do so. Since Tom's business hours are regular during most of the cherished "summer laxity," Janet and the children forgo it so that the family may eat breakfast together, but they then sit in at the Adams' breakfast after Tom has departed for the day.

The habit of "sitting close" has clung. When they were first married, Janet and Tom sat side by side at table. When the children arrived, other arrangements had to be made in order to help two babies. But, at the oval table, the family ranges on one side together, and forms a united front in facing any guests. Thus expediency is not permitted to interfere any more than is possible with the basic meaning of their seating arrangements.

Though the two parts of the family eat separately now, all "celebrations" (holiday and anniversary meals) are eaten together in one of their apartments, and Saturday lunch is always in the Adams' dining room.

In none of the homes was there a ritualistic observance of class distinction between servants and employers, nor to any great extent a similar attitude toward division of labor. In Mr. Adams' family, the hired girl sat at table except when there was company. The sisters took care of their rooms, even little brother learned to cook and "is proud of a skill that he developed as a hobby." The servants in Mrs. Adams' family were "a responsibility." At the time of the freeing of the slaves, her family (which would never deal in buying or selling human beings, but had inherited a number of them) gave the slaves their choice of leaving or of remaining on the old terms. Even though they could not be paid "wages" many of them preferred to remain, and thus became family responsibilities which could not be dismissed. Mrs. Adams' mother, however, taught her daughter how to cook. Her family took over the serving of certain meals to free the servants, and Mrs. Adams herself ritualized the baking of "celebration" cakes, and the serving of "snacks" for her father. In Tom's home, servants were considered a convenience when they were needed, and not a serious part of conscious social-class ritual. Thus, since all these people have been living together, servants have figured only as the "day's work" variety. The family does the work together, even the children "like to play at helping. . . ." In this process of working together, new family forms spring up and are consolidated with older ones of the Adams family.

B. *Family Recreation:*

MR. ADAMS:

Our home evenings were very delightful, I thought, after I was old enough to be allowed to stay up. There was music always, and every week or two there were charades, dialogues, and playlets. We kept quite a supply of old clothes and "fixings" in the attic so that we could "dress up" for these occasions. There were no movies and no auto, of course, during my childhood in the Middle West.

Father purchased one of the earliest parlor organs brought to that part of the country and taught himself to play it with the aid of an instruction book which came along in the purchase. Although he bought a piano for the girls, he preferred the organ, and his favorite compositions were Civil War songs, which he played upon the black keys. There were, however, many lively duos with Father at the organ and my oldest sister at the piano. This sister, eight years plus my senior, became quite an accomplished pianist. It was she who taught me to play, largely out of self-defense, at a very early age. I was always present when she practiced, and at the close of her practice period, she would take me onto her lap. My tendency, as is with all children, I believe, was toward modernistic harmonies produced with the flat of the hand. To avoid this, she guided my fingers over tiny tunes and was as surprised as anyone else to discover after a short period of time that I could play the tunes. I was later given lessons by a regular teacher and we were going along in fine style until she made the unfortunate mistake of telling me she did not believe in Santa Claus. From that time until I was grown, Sister and I battled it out together ever and anon.

MRS. ADAMS:

Our regularized entertainments at home were family gatherings during which times we read aloud, played games, made candy and popped corn.

JANET:

Reading aloud was always our chief family entertainment. This included reading of plays, often by parts. Some part of every evening and Sunday was so spent. Of all our customs connected with recreation, this reading was the most important ritual. Dad played for us when the mood struck him, especially some new composition of his own. Upon the completion of each such endeavor, we were all invited into his studio. While we had heard it grow, maintained the unusual quiet in the house, the hushed meals with Dad distracted, this was our first "official hearing." It was followed by much hilarity and a family celebration. Radio figured only incidentally with us.

TOM:

There were no regular family entertainment rituals.

CHILDREN:

They are just the same as they were for Janet.

Comments

Mr. and Mrs. Adams' family recreation consisted of home-improvised diversions, as was characteristic of their generation of autobiographers living under similar circumstances. There were not many places to go, no easy ways to get there. They did not describe these affairs as formal rituals (although Mr. Adams did to a greater extent than did his wife) but rather as what one did evenings. And what one did was not only diverting but educational—in the narrow, as well as in the broad, sense of the word. Music, plays, and games were the attractions in Mr. Adams' home (it is interesting to note that he describes as recreation ritual the sister-brother piano-playing times which ultimately led to his professional career), and in Mrs. Adams' it was reading aloud and games—though music, in the form of singing, entered into her family rites at bedtime. In Janet's home with her parents, the forces which have attracted many of her generation outside of the home did not operate very strongly upon the combination of these two systems. Janet was early indoctrinated into the reading-aloud, musical, game-playing atmosphere, and enjoyably so. She entered it rather precociously at a near-adult level and the educational aspect became strengthened. It may be significant that Janet was so rapid in her advancement at school that her father finally set an age limit before which she could not leave high school, and even after that she was sent to a school of acting for a year before entering college, where she was the youngest in her class. Acquiring knowledge is "fun" in this household, and enters into many of their formal rituals. Although Janet does not mention it, the observer has noted that at social functions in their home now, charades are very likely to be a part of the evening's entertainment, as are games of other kinds. It is Mr. Adams who presides over the charades (which were a part of his childhood ritual), and all members join in inventing new games to amuse the guests. Guessing games center around famous literary and musical characters. The singing of songs and piano-playing are prominent. To sum it up: there has been a gradual accumulation, enrichment, and crystallization of ritual elements brought in from both sides of the family.

Something new has been added, however. Tom has introduced an automobile to the family, and also bought a television set. As Janet puts it:

I married a husband and a car. The primary effect of it has been to make it easier to get to the few places we always went to anyway—such as seeing the rhododendrons on Memorial Day. The car has also instituted a few new, now-set customs: taking Sunday afternoon drives; seeing the dogwood at Valley Forge and the cherry blossoms in Fairmount Park each spring. And it may change our summer vacation habits. (To this she adds: "Doubtful." See pages 171-172.)

As for the television set. Tom bought it because the children saw one at a neighbor's home and wanted to go see the pictures. We don't like frequent entertainments that aren't home-centered. So the television set arrived—and it also makes going to the movies unnecessary. There are always certain programs that we all watch, and these have been decided upon by mutual agreement of everyone's liking them. Very important, though, are the baseball games. Whenever one starts, the set is turned on. We do not all stop our work to watch, but drift in and out as we please. There is, however, one person always stationed at the television set, who gives the signal whenever the game gets very exciting, and who always keeps track of the score and reports to the rest of us. Sometimes this is Catharine, because she is not engaged in work, and she is well able to tell the score at any moment, as well as the innings and how many hits, etc.

C. *Bedtime:*

Mr. Adams considered the "family evening" as the bedtime ritual and recalled no further specific forms.

Mrs. Adams:

While we were very small, Daddy came after we were ready for bed and sang us to sleep. After that, he read to us till we fell asleep. If he was forced to be away from home, Mother told us stories.

Janet:

Mother always sang last thing, several songs. Bedtime was very ritualistic. After the dishes we played games, or started reading aloud at once, in either case we read aloud before time to go to bed. Dad did the great bulk of the reading, but Mother rested him some, and as soon as I could read, I was given my turns. Especial attention was given to proper reading, ennunciation, emphasis, interpretation, proper breathing, etc., so that it constituted training in public reading and speaking. Voice control, pitch, volume, development of carrying quality were all stressed.

The material read was this: There were the classics, of course, Scott (entire), Cooper, Dickens, Shakespeare, Longfellow, Byron, Browning (poetry was very much present as were plays), but equally prominent were history, mythology, and religion. We considered a good historical text (not just a textbook but the treatment of a particular theme, or a biography) a particular treat. Cyrus, Cambyses, Darius, etc., were the objects of my childhood wonder and imagination. By religion, I do not mean just Bible reading, or Christian doctrine, but the great religious works and ideas of all ages and places. I had the great religious literature of the world read to me.

After the reading, Mother took me to bed. When I was all bathed and dressed for bed, I knelt beside the bed and said my prayers, while Mother listened. Then she tucked me in, kissed me, and put out the light.

Tom:

No bedtime rituals.

CHILDREN (as reported by Janet):

They are pretty much the same as mine. Reading (after a romp) very much the same books as were read to me at their age. Last of all I sing, always ending with "Onward Christian Soldiers," the children's own preference. Also, I usually sing "Rockaby Baby," Brahms' Lullaby (in German), and one song appropriate to the season, as a Christmas Carol, The Palms, the Holy City, etc.

Comments

Obviously, Janet's rituals represent a complete blending of the experiences of both her parents, with emphasis on her mother's. The parents are both teachers. The educational aspect became more pointed in their family in respect to general knowledge, with specific training in qualities of voice control, pitch, etc., so important to the ear of a sensitive musician. The songs used in Janet's and in the present generation are not those produced out of a superficial and ephemeral cultural moment, but ones that have lived and have meaning to a series of generations. Already, at three and four, the children are becoming familiar with "living" literature and songs, of the kind that they can pass down to their own children, and they have started on the course to "conversing in a foreign language part of each day" by at least hearing the Lullaby in German each night. Tom enters actively into all these rituals, only very occasionally feeling that he is becoming a bit "orthodox." Recently he has been baptized and confirmed in the church to which the whole family go. Since then, he has led the family prayer at the children's bedtime. Janet feels that it will be only a short time now before he will take over the table blessing, once more restoring that ritual to its proper form.

D. *Farewells:*

MR. ADAMS:

When one member left the house, there were kisses all around for the family, and those remaining behind ushered the departing one to the door. There were waves and parting admonishings from the front porch if the weather permitted, otherwise from the windows.

Mrs. Adams:

No one ever left home without goodby. Kisses all around; brother and I, if we did not go together, always watched each other out of sight. Mother was with the watcher if possible.

Janet:

We always kissed everyone at home before leaving, and those who remained waved from the porch or door in warm weather, the window in cold, until the departee was out of sight. The one leaving always waved back. There were "hurry home," "be good," "be careful," etc.

Tom:

No rituals. Just left the house.

Children:

Same as Janet's.

Comments

In the present generation, this ritual appears to be almost constant and very much formalized. With four adults coming and going, for work, for shopping, etc., there are many times a day when this formal farewell takes place. Everyone in the house who is aware of a departure participates in this, even if the departure is only a matter of going to the corner store. The children have even included neighbors in this rite if the neighbor happens to be leaving his home when the babies are at the windows or in the yard. They always call out the neighbor's name, sometimes ask where he is going, and always wave him goodby with big smiles, until out of sight. Tom adopted this ritual completely even before marriage, while visiting the Adamses. He has been teased about it by his own family, but is not daunted.

E. *Discipline:*

Mr. Adams:

Punishments were not frequent in our family, and such as they were consisted in being sent to bed, with meager meals, pleasures denied, etc. I was rarely, if ever, spanked, not because I didn't need it, but I think it was because my parents were afraid I would fall apart if spanked.

MRS. ADAMS:

Disapproval and admonition were the only disciplines we knew. I believe an occasional spank was used when we were too young to remember.

JANET:

In our small, close-knit family, disapproval was almost always sufficient. If not, omission of evening reading, or cut of allowance might follow.

TOM:

Spanking, always and for everything.

CHILDREN:

On rare occasions, spanking, being sent to bed, sitting on chairs, etc. But almost everything is best handled by a serious talk from their mother.

Comments

Discipline in all parts of the family but Tom's was not very formally ritualized. It was experimental, suited to the individual child and the particular offense. With Tom, it was a set ritual. His children are subjected to the experimental methods of discipline. While they are still very young, spanking does figure to a minor extent, but already it is the feeling of disfavor with the family that is coming to be most impressive to these children. (Upon one occasion, when the observer received a gift from Tommy, then two years old, she cried, "What did you do, Tommy?" Tommy dissolved into tears. This was the expression used by his family when he had been naughty.) Already this method is sufficient for the little girl, and Janet prophesies that, in another year, spankings will be a thing of the past for Tommy also.

F. *Vacations:*

Mr. Adams mentions no vacation rituals.

MRS. ADAMS:

There was no set custom. More often than anything else, we went to the mountains in the summer. Mother, Brother and I would go for a prolonged stay, and Daddy would join us when he could. Long journeys were not taken together, and were determined by circumstances. We all traveled at times.

JANET:
At home together, reading and working together at household repairs we didn't have time to make during the rest of the year.

TOM:
Away from home, apart. Mother and/or some of the five who were hers often went to A——.

CHILDREN:
Same as Janet's.

Comments

There was never much emphasis on ritualizing away-from-home summer vacations in any of the various parts of the family, though the grandparent generation did occasionally travel and go on vacation, as did Tom's family. Even these sporadic excursions have disappeared in Janet's and her children's homes. Home is the best place to be, and in summer there is opportunity for constructive work that cannot be accomplished jointly by busy people during the regular work-winter. Tom is particularly skilled in construction and repair, and shares this skill with Mr. Adams, who also makes a hobby of furniture-making and refinishing. The first warm days of spring are the inevitable signal for these two to appear at some such project, and it continues all summer, with the rest of the family participating always with suggestions, fetching tools, etc., even down to the children, who are constantly under foot.

It is interesting to note that Janet felt that the car, introduced by Tom, was about to make a change in their vacation habits. Tom was more used to going away for a while than was Janet. Furthermore, Tom's business provides several weeks for vacation, instead of the whole summer which Mrs. Adams' work provides. Each year since they have been married, Tom and Janet have tentatively planned to drive somewhere during this time, but have not yet quite got off. In this, the fifth year of their marriage, they were again planning such a trip.

While going over the notes on this study, they made a discovery. Janet had thought that Tom liked to take a vacation. Tom thought Janet wanted a change and to see some of her relatives. Both of them actually preferred keeping to the usual summer habits. Such was the adjustment process of one part of family life!

H. *Naming:*
Mr. Adams:

The custom was to choose several favorite names in each generation of my family and to use them over and over again till children stopped coming. This meant that when the family was large, brothers or sisters sometimes had the exact same names. They were distinguished by using nicknames for them.

Mrs. Adams:

In my family, every woman names her first girl for her own mother, using her husband's mother's name for a middle name if she wishes; her second girl for herself, complete; the third girl for her mother-in-law (unless included in the middle name of the first). The first boy is named for the child's father; the second, for the maternal grandfather; the third, for the paternal grandfather (unless a duplicate of the first child's name).

Grandparents are *never* called "grandmother" or "grandfather." It isn't considered quite proper. The first child in a family is encouraged to choose some name for his grandparents, and this name clings. Ancestors of some generations back are referred to subsequently by their child-chosen names, even by family members who were born long after they died.

Janet:

Though I have some favorite names for children, I won't be able to use them unless I have a very large family, because the first six are already named. The two I have are, of course, Catharine, after my mother, and Tommy, after his father. Catharine has long since chosen the nicknames for my mother and father, by which they will be remembered by future generations.

Comments

The strong traditions of Mrs. Adams' family in naming had little competition from the confusing system of Mr. Adams' family, and none at all from Tom's family. The emphasis upon proper naming, however, developed into a second kind of custom in Janet's generation. The family has always had domestic animals as pets. All dogs were labeled with human names, and cats with names from classical antiquity, real or mythological. The children have so far had two dogs, Teddy and Lucy, and two cats, Wenceslaus and Eros. It is to be noted also that certain names reappear in the animal part of the family as well as in the human part. There have been recently, for instance, four Teddys and two Haroun-al-Raschids.

I. *Religious Rituals:*

MR. ADAMS:

When I was a very young child our church life was rather strenuous. All cooking and baking for Sunday was done on Saturday, and Saturday was bath night, and how!

Our Sunday schedule usually started an hour later than on weekdays. All conversation was carried on in undertones or whispers and nothing was discussed or planned that could wait until Monday. The parlor curtains were drawn at half mast and the furniture was so polished that it formed a hazard for careless flies. The church was only four blocks away, and we walked unless the weather was too bad. We sallied solemnly forth, Indian file, Father took the lead, his Van Dyke tilted at just the proper angle; Mother bustled along second in her bustles and black alpaca. Being the youngest, I, of course, brought up the rear. [Mrs. Adams, in interview, told the observer that in her family the children had to walk ahead of their parents on the way to church. When asked what she did with her own child in this respect, she answered, "Well, Janet walked between us, because she was only one. But if my mother had been with us, Janet would have preceded us!"]

The service and Sunday School lasted three or four hours, at the conclusion of which we filed solemnly home again and feasted upon the food cooked the day before. After dinner the grown-ups slept or read, appropriate literature, of course. Father generally slept and I remember wondering that he did not have a Sunday snore. It seemed to me that his Sunday snore was fully as loud, if not more so than on weekdays. I considered the question quite seriously but never got around to asking about it. The children were also expected to read quietly or sleep on Sunday afternoons, but as we grew older and more restless, we were allowed a few quiet games with the window shades down.

All of our people were baptized, became church members and

were married by ministers in the home. Funeral services were also conducted from the homes.

MRS. ADAMS:

Grace at meals; family prayers; bedtime prayers; Bible readings. Daddy always presided. If he was away, Mother took his place.

Daddy was active in religious work, and I was always with him from the time I could walk. We always attended service on Sunday, and any other that his time or inclination dictated. Mother and brother joined us when they cared to.

We always had a special midday dinner with service on the sideboard for any guests who might be brought home, and we always released all the help from dinnertime on, and provided for ourselves in the evening.

Members were not married in church or confirmed in church. They got married by a minister and were baptized in church. They did not have church funerals, though it was necessary for my father because there were so many people who had a right to want to be there that the home was not large enough to admit them.

JANET:

Grace (the "Blessing" we always called it) was always the beginning of every meal. I was grown before I knew how else anyone would know when to start eating. Dad always asked it, except on those rare occasions when he was away; then Mother officiated. Bedtime prayers were equally routine, the bath might be missed, the prayers never. We read the New Testament, Psalms, Proverbs, and rarely the Pentateuch. Occasionally the Apochrypha also. I received a Testament at six and a Bible at ten, a family custom. I not only read, I memorized the Bible, whole chapters at a chunk! A reward would be offered me for completion of such and such a chapter. When I could go through it from memory without prompting, I got the reward. I learned, read, and recited on the lives of the religious great of all religions.

We usually attended church; where depended on what organ Dad was playing at the moment. My family put me in a Friends' school because they wanted me to have religious instruction without denominational dogma, and later joined the Society for the same reason. Then I attended Bible school in the summer. I was sent for special instruction in biblical history, exegesis, higher criticism, etc. Such a religious groundwork was traditional in Mother's family. "Learn all you can about every faith," was regarded as the best guard against error, and a stimulus to thought. In our family the one error was not knowing what you believed and why. Anything else was tolerated.

On Sundays our meals were different, and there was more time for reading, discussions, etc.

We are always married at home, in a trainless gown, and by a minister, because marriage is considered a sacrament whose vows are religious in nature.

TOM:

No grace or family prayers. Always attended First Day School and Meeting.

On Sunday, we slept or went out. As to sacraments—the Friends do not have these, and marriage in church was strictly optional.

CHILDREN (as reported by Janet):

They are the same as mine, except that I ask the blessing now. The children are in the Church Nursery School; we go to church. Religious education is centered in the home, though, and will follow the pattern of my own.

On Sunday we take an afternoon drive in the car, have later meals (often only two), and do more reading aloud.

Observance and attitudes about sacraments would not be altered from generation to generation since it is a "tribal" concern, not a matter of indiscriminate family opinion.

Comments

Mr. Adams' family represents old-style orthodox rituals, descending upon the family members in toto, with some leeway for growing, restless children. Mrs. Adams' family, on the other hand, did not present just the same kind of relentlessly orthodox picture. Her father was active in religious work, and Mrs. Adams always went with him to church on Sunday. Her mother and brother, however, came along when they chose. Janet reports that a good groundwork of non-denominational religious instruction was traditional in this side of the family, and it should be recalled that Janet is now a lecturer in Comparative Religion. It was Mrs. Adams' father who presided over the orthodox forms in the household, and her mother who created the atmosphere of a Sunday at home which was less confiningly heavy than that in Mr. Adams' home. This does not mean that religion and its rituals were less important to Mrs. Adams' side of the family. Indeed, religion was stressed as a great responsibility. One had to be instructed in all religions and in their rites, in order to make an intelligent choice and to participate conscientiously. As Janet has said: "In our family the one error was not knowing what you believed and why." This includes a conscientiousness about all ritualistic forms in which one does believe.

When Mr. and Mrs. Adams made their own home with Janet, the attitudes and atmosphere passed down by Mrs. Adams' mother remained. Many of the little orthodox forms such as prayers, grace, etc., which had been presided over by her father, and also existed in Mr. Adams' home, also survived. But the exclusive sectarian tone dropped out to give way to a broader interpretation of religion and family responsibility toward it. General social change, as well as the direct matriarchal influence that has become apparent, may have been influential here. Mr. Adams' profession (including playing the church organ) added to the exposure to different churches. Tom, on his part well prepared for non-denominational emphasis in the Society of Friends, has contributed the secular ritual of the Sunday afternoon drive. He is now a member of the church to which the whole family currently goes—an Episcopal church. These different ways of thinking and behaving in respect to religion have resulted in present-day rituals which express a religious attitude that is serious, but not narrow; an attitude of responsibility that is educating and interesting even to small children, rather than tiresome and deadening to them. The family has preserved all forms which accommodate to these attitudes, and has discarded those that do not.

J. *Holiday Rituals:*
MR. ADAMS:

Our relatives were numerous, and on Christmas and the Fourth we all stayed together for two or three days, the children being bedded down upon blankets on the floor at night. There were sometimes thirty-odd at these gatherings, and meals were served at the first, second, and third tables.

We had a family orchestra for these parties. One of my cousins played the fiddle, another an accordion, and an uncle was a "whiz" on the harmonica. Father played the organ, Sister the piano and I played the drums. Sounds like the Morgan Family in the old song, doesn't it?

MRS. ADAMS:

We did all of it at Christmas time ["all of it" means the exact Christmas ritual as described by Janet below]. We often, but not invariably, went to a sunrise service, after seeing what Santa Claus had left in stockings and on trees. We set the stage for him on Christmas Eve. Then home to breakfast. Then out to carry gifts to friends and relatives—see their gifts and exchange greetings. Then home to the traditional Christmas dinner of fresh pork, fowl, yams, cranberries, fruit salad, mince pie, nuts, candies—it never varied.

Thanksgiving we celebrated in the usual way—church service, turkey dinner, guests, etc.

On Easter Saturday, we dyed eggs—then all of the children who played together went out to an open space, built a fire under a huge kettle on a tripod, and boiled eggs until no one would eat another egg. We took bread and butter, cold meats (if we wanted them) and anything else we might want to eat with the eggs. We exchanged colored eggs with our friends on Easter morning.

Everybody's birthday was observed by gifts and special dinner—guests were not always present, but more frequently than not.

Valentines were always exchanged with each other and with friends. The day was observed by having heart-shaped cakes, something red in the ice-cream, heart-shaped candies, etc.

Hallowe'en was always occasion for a party, usually costumed, but was a group celebration, not a family one.

JANET:

Christmas began and still begins with the Thanksgiving holidays. From then on each of us has a closet, drawer, room or some place that is sacrosanct and inviolable for the hiding of presents. Special times are reserved for family trips into town to see the decorations, etc., aside from individual shopping trips. We always went the rounds of the better-known churches at this season. A week before-hand the house is decorated extensively with holly and mistletoe and what other ornaments appeal to us at that season. Once hung, they are never changed. Mistletoe is always in a doorway, the Golden Bough insuring return. Some gifts may be wrapped in advance, but one or more must be left for Christmas Eve, which is our really big time, more so than Christmas. The day begins with an especially heavy breakfast, because it will be the last formally prepared meal until dinner the next day. In the morning everybody scurries in and out making last-minute purchases of cards, tags, seals, etc., of which there is usually an abundance anyway. We just like them. The afternoon, usually considered to begin when the last one of us came in from the last trip out, is spent in scurrying at home, seeing that all presents were ready and available for the evening's ceremonies (that tree ornaments were present and in order, etc.). Supper was an informal meal, eaten together standing or sitting in the kitchen, whenever everybody could stop for a few minutes. This was early, to leave plenty of time for the evening's ritual. After a catch-as-catch-can supper (the food is left out for "nibbling" through the evening, which often extends to 10 or 11 P.M. for children and usually 2 or 3 A.M. for adults) the real celebration begins. We all go out and carry in the tree, which serves us as Yule Log also, though not burned. Until tree shortage forced its earlier purchase, the selecting and buying of the tree was left to this time. The tree is carried to its selected standing place by every member of the family big enough to walk. It is carried to the accompaniment of traditional songs, which are continued until the base is attached and the tree stands in place. Then the Yule-tide is toasted in the wassail-cup, usually egg-nog, the preparation of which was part of the after-noon's work. Then the ornaments are brought out and hung, accom-panied by carol-singing. Each member in turn, beginning with the oldest, goes to the ornament box, selects one, and puts it on the tree. After the first round, everybody just pitches in and decorates. A few ornaments have come down through a great many years, and occupy a traditional place on the tree. A Santa figure and a reindeer always sit under the tree, and a church, which, being less durable, is replaced from time to time.

When the tree is trimmed, we all stand around it and sing through most of the traditional carols. Then the little folks who have no packages to wrap go to bed to wait for Santa Claus. Before they go, each receives one of the candy canes that are always part of the tree trimming and one present from the grown-ups. All presents from outside the household have been unwrapped as they arrived, and are now crowded together to one side of the tree. When a child is old enough to have wrapping to do, it stays up for the next part of the "service," but goes to bed before Santa's presents arrive. After the tree trimming, we all scatter, each to a room he or she had selected, into which no one else may go from supper on, where each has spread out gifts, wrappings, etc. Then the presents are wrapped and decorated. No one emerges until all are finished. Then we all come out carrying the presents which we place on or under the tree according to size and weight. Finally, Santa's presents, not wrapped, emerge from hiding, and are placed in a semicircle around the front of the tree. Again the Yule is toasted, coffee passed, and the food in the kitchen liberally raided. Then comes the moment of "first gifts." Dad goes to the tree and selects one package to open that evening. He opens it and after it has been duly admired,

Mother takes her turn, then I; since my marriage, my husband follows me. After the first gifts are opened, anyone who especially wants any member to open any particular thing so indicates. Usually about half the presents for the grown-ups are opened that night. One last round of carols is sung, and we all go to bed.

Christmas morning everybody gets up when the first one gets awake and goes for the others with "Merry Christmas. Christmas gift. Santa has come." We all return to the tree, and following the order of the night before, we open presents. Recipients of gifts from Santa are exempt from order, and are expected to discover and claim their own at once. Coffee is served the adults.

After the presents, comes breakfast, heavy, but eaten in a flurry. As soon as it is over, dinner is begun. Everybody works on it, as on all meals, so Christmas is a big kitchen day for the family. Even visitors or invited guests are served coffee in the kitchen as soon as they have seen the tree and the presents. All children visitors are given canes off the tree.

Christmas dinner comes in the early to middle afternoon. We always have fresh pork, usually a shoulder, and paschal celery. After dinner there are the nuts, dates, and figs from the stockings. The stockings, always including a red-and-black one with bells on it that has been in the family for generations, are hung on Christmas Eve, at the time the tree is trimmed, for Santa to leave nuts and fruits in them, always including some over-sized oranges and grapefruit for Christmas breakfast and through Christmas week, and the nuts, dates and figs. Dessert is always plum pudding, although there may also be a mince pie. We never go to church on Christmas, unless Dad is playing an organ.

Thanksgiving is celebrated at home. We usually have fowl for dinner, and when I was little we usually heard an opera sometime during the four days. Later we took to listening to the football game (Pennsylvania-Cornell) and still do.

Easter: Hot Cross Buns for Good Friday. Easter Eve we make a bunny nest which is filled with candy eggs, chocolate and colored, and eggs dyed and decorated the night before, some of which are cooked for breakfast. We exchange minor presents and Dad always supplies a colorful flowering plant,

New Year's Eve: always an open house with our friends, we always toast the New Year in egg-nog. However, except for our enjoyment of the party with our friends, New Year's is the least important of all the gala feasts.

Washington's Birthday: table decorated with hatchets, cherries, pictures of George and Martha Washington, cherry pie for dessert, and chocolate cherries for candy.

Valentine's Day: a big celebration. We exchange presents, not the very big ones, but jewelry, perfumes, stockings, etc.; give each other Valentines, have special cakes and candies and a festive dinner with decorated table. We frequently have a party on the nearest weekend.

St. Patrick's Day: another big one. We have the green feathers for girls and women and little hats for the men, and the little Sinn-Fein Shamrock pins. Dinner is begun with the singing of "The Wearin' o' The Green." The meal is typically Irish, followed by green mints and cinnamon potatoes. The table is decorated in the green, across which is laid one orange band. Each member has worn green, or some symbolic green emblem all day. At dinner each of us is dressed as nearly as possible in green. The table talk revolves around Ireland's struggles for independence, and the deeds and exploits of various Irish-Patriot ancestors; these are detailed at least this one time each year, so that there is no chance that the memory might grow dim. After dinner, we dance the jig, the Morris Dances, and the Sword Dance, which, though Scottish, was taken into Ireland by those Highlandmen who would not bow to British rule, and went over to continue the fight. (This was my father's side of the family. Mother's Irish ancestry was really Irish in origin, and hence the one orange band on the table.) We sing traditional Irish and Highland songs, and then recall and recount the exploits of the Scotch ancestors.

April Fool's Day: just family fun.

May Day Eve: as a child I always went out with the tiny candles to see the flowers put to bed, and light the way for the little people. In the morning I went back to look for fairy rings, and perchance to catch a fairy (and get a wish) in a morning glory. The dew of May morning had special magic, etc.

Memorial Day: go to see the rhododendrons.

Midsummer Night is observed.

July Fourth is a family party.

August 24th is Mother's and Dad's wedding anniversary. When they get up, Dad goes down to the piano and plays " 'Tis Thy Wedding Morning," from *The Rosemaiden* (since my own marriage, he has done the same for me). Presents for the "bride" or household gifts for the couple are presented at breakfast, unless someone has to hurry off, then they are saved for dinner, which is a big, festive one, with flowers. The whole day is in party mood.

Birthdays: same pattern as anniversaries, except "Happy Birthday" replaces *The Rosemaiden*. For the children there is a birthday party on the Sunday preceding their real birth date, if that does not fall on a Sunday.

Hallowe'en: the house is decorated. We often have a party, and always a special dinner ending in pumpkin pie, spice wafers, and cider, nuts, etc. We always keep special supplies for "beggars."

Tom:

Christmas: Mother had all the close relatives of both husbands for dinner. There was always a tree, decorated by whoever got time, and presents. Always turkey for dinner. Always Christmas cards sent out by the family.

Thanksgiving: turkey and all the assorted relatives.

Easter: ignored.

New Year's: each member went out on his or her own, if old enough. Otherwise, to bed.

Birthdays were celebrated by a party of the friends of the one having it, not always by the rest of the family, unless they shared the same friends.

No others: we were not a "celebrating" family.

Children (as reported by Janet):

All those dropped out as I outgrew them have been revived for my children, will be dropped as they grow up, and resumed again when they (certainly Catharine and to a lesser degree Tommy) have children. When he marries, Tommy will probably come into a new set of rituals (his wife's) into which ours will be fitted as they do not conflict, but Catharine must and will transmit them intact, to a daughter of her own (Janet), and so on.

Comments

In the present generation, holidays evidence the epitome of the rituals of this family, embodying a collection of the experiences of the generations and expressing all the important elements contained in others of the present-day rites. Some of these elements are: the whole family together; recalling the past; using tangible objects handed down from the past; making use of accumulated rich knowledge; teaching the younger generation and new family members both the forms and the content, much of which is of an enduring cultural type; improvising as they go along and consolidating many of these improvisations; insisting upon absolute observance; maintaining a balance between the serious responsibility of perpetuation and having fun while doing so. "A snowball accumulation" truly describes the rolling downhill through generations of customs and traditions that have resulted in the current family holiday rites. Particles that have broken off in the snowball's course have done so because they could not possibly adhere, or because they warped the smooth shaping of the whole. The Adams cannot "bed down" thirty relatives for holidays when the relatives are now scattered in far parts of the country, but the two separate family units can merge for every holiday to celebrate, though their number comes only to six. They cannot perpetuate a family orchestra for want of performers, but they can all sing and enjoy the piano; and the heritage from the musical side of the family is thus preserved and ritualized in changed form.

Observations on the Ritual Process in the Family Study

The continuities which occur in the Adams family rituals seem to rest upon certain factors characteristic of the group and the individuals within it.

1. Most marked is the strong tradition of matriarchy in Mrs. Adams' side of the family. This could be maintained in an unbroken line, because the family did have at least one daughter in each generation. (Janet remarks that it would be a tragedy in her family not to have a daughter.)

2. The tradition of matriarchy includes a conscious responsibility of perpetuation of family forms and customs.

3. Perpetuation is facilitated by the possession of tangible objects (heirlooms) which are handed down by ritualized rules and reinforce the consciousness of having ancestors, and the memory of their names and natures.

4. Much of the intangible content of the rituals (such as songs, literature, games, etc.) is of a culturally enduring nature, and neither closely age- nor time-delimited.

5. Both Mrs. Adams and Janet were only daughters (at present, Catharine is also). Since not too much is expected of men as carriers of family heritage, this responsibility has probably taken on especial emphasis in the cases of these two people. This is marked throughout Janet's conversations as recorded, both as concerns her own firm attitudes toward the

strict observance of her rituals and her feelings about training Catharine for her responsibility.

6. The type of mate selected in this family has aided in the strengthening of the rites. Janet feels that this is circular in cause and effect. A woman of her family would not be attracted to the kind of man who would not enjoy and fit into the ritualized atmosphere of their home, and she would have ample opportunity to discover this while he was subjected to it before marriage. Be that as it may, the fact is that both Mr. Adams and Tom, from different ritual backgrounds and varying much from each other's, are active and equal participants along with the others—not just sideline observers.

7. No one is permitted the opportunity of developing rebellion to the rituals. But this is gently effected. All members are quite articulate and outspoken, and the needs and wishes of each individual are justly considered. This is a family spirit, and does not reach the stage of formal family council. The rituals are therefore so arranged that everyone has an important and enjoyable part, even the small babies.

Innovations enter the family rituals in two ways:

1. New members come to the family through marriage and birth, and each immediately becomes an accepted and worthy part of the prime value in this home: the whole family group. This is not a woman-against-man matriarchy, but a mother-guardian-and-developer matriarchy. Thus any contributions offered by new members that will enrich the total are eagerly accepted and preserved. This keeps the ritual dynamic and also facilitates interest and participation by the new members. Children, of course, are the super value, and as such any contributions they make are most important.

2. Exigencies of daily living together, professional routines, new inventions, new knowledge, new philosophies, all give rise to experimentation. As these experiments satisfy and do not conflict with cherished values they are incorporated as parts of the ritual structure.

Discontinuities show up to no great extent in this study, probably because they are relatively few, and also because those that may have occurred are difficult to trace after they have been lost. The strong matriarchal family line insists upon preserving its own traditions; Mr. Adams' family rituals were largely harmonious; and Tom's family's absence of ritual offered little chance for discovered discontinuities from this source. Some forms, however, have been noted as lost.

1. This has occurred chiefly through sheer necessity, as when the personnel is absent, or does not have a particular talent required to perpetuate a rite.

2. The time when many small forms may be lost (when small children outgrow them) is bridged to a great extent in this case, partly by good memory and conscious revival, but even more, the observer believes, by the fact that *all* rituals in this home are *integrated* into one system—each carrying along many important elements of the others. They are all based upon the same attitudes and philosophies and goals. These, and many of the forms attendant to them, keep constantly reappearing throughout the rituals. Thus it is comparatively simple to fit a new child into them, as his mother had been before him, by a temporary simplification suited to childlike needs. The outstanding example of this is the Christmas ritual. Being as much a grown-up rite as a child's rite, and maintaining the same forms, it does not alter when a new child arrives, nor are old customs for children forgotten.

Summary

The study of the rituals of three generations in one family has revealed certain processes in the dynamics of family ritual. This family is not presented as typical of "The American Family" nor are its specific rituals considered to be usual. Certain aspects of the ritual process in this family, however, may be pertinent for more general projection:

Rituals may tend to survive through combinations of the following factors in family life:

1. when the rituals are all integrated into one family ritual system which represents the enduring attitudes, philosophies, and goals of the whole family group—rather than a discon-

nected series of separate forms serving the temporal needs and pleasures of certain individual family members.

2. when these attitudes, philosophies, and goals are expressed in forms which also provide rich sensate content (sounds, sights, smells, tastes), physical exercise, mental stimulus, and, in general, "good fun."

3. when material family objects are handed down along with their histories and are included frequently in the rituals.

4. when the intangible content of the rituals consists of enduring cultural values, rather than cultural "passing fancies."

5. when this content is not too strictly age-delimited.

6. when the family lives in a home which is adequate in size for whole-family participation in elaborate ritualizing.

7. when there is an unbroken family line (in this case matriarchal, as is the case of a large proportion of American families) to receive the rites, the content, and to pass them on.

8. when there is the momentum of several generations behind their observance, and a feeling of pride in, or responsibility for, their perpetuation.

9. when rituals are all-family inclusive, with equal satisfaction for all members, precluding attack from non-participants and rebellion from a participant.

10. when there is an active acceptance of newcomers into the family, and when their contributions are incorporated gently into the integrated whole wherever possible.

11. when experimentation is permitted, and results which do not break the integration are incorporated to contribute novelty, fresh interest, and improved service.

Rituals may tend to disappear when the opposite of all, or combinations, of these conditions exist. They may also perish through:

1. the loss of personnel.

2. removal from the site of a ritual.

3. social change which makes old rituals seem peculiar or obsolete.

4. the joining of individuals from ritual systems which are absolutely incompatible.

Family Ritual and Family Integration

THE PRESENT chapter seeks to bring together the main segments of our conclusions in the present study, and to formulate them into a thesis concerning the overall importance of ritual in family living. It is hoped that this thesis, if justified by this and other studies in verification that may be made, will suggest an approach of basic promise in the promotion of better family living.

First, a Brief Recapitulation

1. Our analysis of published autobiographies shows that when mature adults, who have achieved at least a modicum of prominence in the world, view their early family life in retrospect and seek to recapture the essence of the earlier stages of their lives, they do so in large measure in terms of recurrent forms of procedure, i.e., family patterns of behavior which we call family rituals. As stated in Chapter 4, these rituals framed the canvas revealing each family, and within which single events and crises came to have their specific meaning. These rituals have the attributes of frequent repetition, of being social in nature, and of having an emotional coloring. Through them, also, much of the family culture was

transmitted to the next generation. To us it is of significance that intelligent persons, from many different walks in life, not trained in sociological lore or anthropological emphases, should agree so generally, not only in the prescribed family patterns they describe, but also in the importance they attribute to them.

2. Family rituals, viewed through the eyes of university students, fall into two groups: Those that carry on family traditions, and those that arise spontaneously to meet a specific situation, do so successfully, and come therefore to be continued. In either event, they are emphasized as indicative of a certain predictability of family and individual behavior, thus easing the stress and strain of group living together; and as instruments in conditioning the behavior of younger members of the family. The analysis of our material shows the molding of many personality traits through the repeated practice of obligatory actions which, taken in combination, tend to develop habits of social stability and adaptability. More specifically, family ritual is related to social habits of coöperation, regularity, punctuality, and recognition of the rights of others, which obviously are significant for intra-group relations in general, and for the family group in particular.

3. Rituals are an integral part of the family culture, hence they vary from one cultural level to another, or from one social class to another. Our studies show marked differences between upper-, middle-, and lower-class segments of the population of a large metropolitan area. Rituals take their shape from the milieu in which they arise. Since they represent, at the time of their origin, efforts to meet specific family situations, they vary as these situations differ from one class level to another. This means that young people reared at different class levels have been exposed to, have participated in, and have been conditioned by, family rituals differing in character and extent.

4. Just as family rituals differ on a class basis, so they vary from one stage in the family history or cycle to another, and for similar reasons. The problems to be met, the proof through experience of how best to meet them, the traditions which develop, and the extent to which prescribed procedures have

"jelled" into rituals, naturally vary from the founding to the aging family, or from the family with small children to that which has matured to a point where it serves as a place to launch the children on their respective careers.

5. And yet there is a stubborn continuity about many rituals. This is revealed quite clearly in Chapter 9, which summarizes a study in which the processes of family ritual innovation, continuity, and discontinuity are traced in the same family through three generations.

Ritual and Interpersonal Relations

Running through all of our material is the fact that ritual is a form of regularized personal relationship for members of the family group. This regularization may involve all the members of the family, such as a national holiday or family anniversary observance. Most of the rituals included in our material are of this kind, anticipating and ordinarily obtaining the coöperation of all of the members of the family.

But rituals also develop between individual members of the family. There are, for example, husband-wife rituals. These begin to develop usually in the newly established family, and especially with the coming of children, but may develop at any stage or in any area of the husband-wife relationship. The sex life of the married couple appears to be ritualized in many families, as the following case will serve to illustrate.

One rainy evening, about the second year of their marriage, Mr. and Mrs. Brett were playing cribbage. As the game went on in a desultory sort of way, the conversation between them took an intimate turn, followed also by various little intimate acts, such as playfully touching each other. Finally, as the regular bedtime hour approached, Mr. Brett suggested sex relations, to which Mrs. Brett acquiesced with more than customary willingness. In the following weeks, several more cribbage games culminated in this manner. In each of these cases, the sexual act had been very satisfactory to both husband and wife. Then followed the experience of several sex relationships without the cribbage preliminary. Soon, without any deliberate planning or formal agreement, the cribbage game came to be the regular preliminary to sex relationships. Gradually, additions came to be made. Mr. Brett brought home Mrs. Brett's favorite flowers, and placed them in a vase near to the cribbage table. Then Mrs. Brett suggested a highball, to be sipped toward the end of the cribbage game. Since she preferred Scotch whiskey, Mr. Brett bought the best Scotch brand, which was reserved for their own use on these cribbage nights. Gradually, each step leading to sex relations between the Bretts has come to be ritualized around the cribbage game, ranging from the first shy references to cribbage to the final consummation. At the time this information was given by the Bretts, fifteen years had passed since the beginning of the cribbage ritual. They say that there are times when sex relations occur without this particular preliminary, but agree that it does not "seem so right" as when they lead up to it via the ritual route.

In somewhat disguised form, this ritual case was then read to a number of married couples, and most of them promptly agreed that some ritualizing of the sex relationship and of the steps leading up to it obtained in their particular case; that is to say, there were certain regularized "right" ways of preparing for sexual intercourse, which, when followed, made for a more satisfactory relationship than when not observed.

At this point, we turned to the literature on marital relations, reviewing carefully the parts dealing with sex adjustment in marriage. To us it seems rather clear that much of the advice and admonition given concerning the importance of love play preceding intercourse really calls for the development of preparatory rituals, i.e., the establishment of "right" ways of physical and emotional preparation. Similarly, many of the complaints of wives of the precipitate behavior of their spouses in the sex relation are really stressing the lack of approved preparatory techniques, which are the essence of ritual.

Quite accidentally, at this stage of our study, we encountered medical practitioners who dealt with problems of sex maladjustment in marriage. From them we obtained confirmations of the role of this ritualizing of sex relations. Particular reference was made to the frequency of complaints by the wife of the absence of preparatory rituals by the male partner, and to the disturbing effects of interruptions or breaks in the established ritual. One man's impotence, for example, was attributed by his professional consultant to a change in the physical setting for coitus which made impossible the maintenance of a long established preparatory ritual.

Just as between husband and wife, so the relations between parent and child may be ritualized. Many of our cases are father-daughter or mother-son rituals. These might be a fruitful source of study for the psychoanalytically minded, Here we must content ourselves with the citation of two simple illustrations:

Frank S. lives in a suburb but maintains his office in the near-by city. Every Saturday since his daughter's twelfth birthday, she takes the suburban train and comes to his office by noon. The two then go to a well-known eating place for lunch. After lunch there is a matinee, football game, or other event. This continued for six years until the daughter left to enter a New England college. On these "dates," father and daughter almost never included another person. Most of the problems involving the daughter's school, social, and family life, were talked over by father and daughter on these occasions.

When Richard was married he and his wife began the custom of going to his parents' home every Sunday for dinner. When the dinner was over Richard and his mother did the dishes. The help of other persons was always rejected. Richard always washed and his mother dried. Each Sunday, he would tease his mother about the same things, pretending to complain about the abundance of dishes and playfully accusing his mother of not having done any dishes since the preceding Sunday. Halfway through the process, his mother heated the coffee and she and Richard sat to sip it, and talk about happenings of the preceding week. When all matters had been discussed, the kitchen chores were finished. Often this task and talk would cover a period of two hours and more. At the end of the period, they would rejoin the others with Richard always telling some fantastic tale of how his mother had exploited him during the interval with work saved up during the preceding week.

Considering the personal relationships described in our case material, what happens in this regularizing of behavior? Four aspects can be identified. First, there is a strong sense of continuity about these relationships. The assumption of the participants is that they will go on and on, being repeated at regular intervals. Second, the relationship becomes standardized, and, like a worn rock, becomes more and more smooth as time goes on. There is the prescribed form and sequence, each step leading to the next with the precision, as it were, of a timetable. Behavior becomes predictable, which makes for ease and comfort in the relationship. Third, the relationship is glamourized. There is the effort to make it attractive, and often to make it impressive. The persons involved seem to say: We like what we are doing, we want to do it well and happily. Finally, the emergence of the ritual and its continuance seems to deepen the relationship. As Dunlap has written recently about the role of ritual: "Faith develops from ritual, rather than ritual from faith. The development of faith from ritual, as an interpretation of ritual, and with further progressive reinterpretations, is obviously consonant with the fact that ritual is a group product."[1]

Ritual and the Cultural Approach to the Family

But rituals are more than patterns of personal relationships. They are procedures which have a purpose: they represent choices and values. They are approved ways of doing and thinking, and this means culture.

The more one succeeds in getting on the inside of families, the more one sees them not as mere units of interacting personalities, but as having each its own distinctive ways of living. These constitute the family culture, and it is one of the signal advances in the recent study of the family that we have come to realize that it, like every social institution, is not only a structure and a process of interaction between different per-

[1] Knight, Dunlap, *Religion: Its Function in Human Life,* New York, McGraw-Hill Book Company, 1946, pp. vi, vii.

sonalities, but has also a content of ideas, sentiments, habits, values, and the like.[2]

The family culture pattern covers the range of family living. It includes marriage and courtship procedures, sex mores, husband-wife relationships, status of men and women, guardianship, parent-child relationships, divorce, disposition of child's earnings, family solidarity, responsibility toward aging parents, attitudes toward extra-marital relationships, use of leisure time, and many other matters.

We have come, as a result of the present study, to think that ritual may be the one best starting point for the study of family culture patterns, just as it has long been recognized as the best point from which to begin the study of religion. Ritual obviously comprises much of the behavior of which we are conscious and of which we definitely approve. As a phase of family life it represents what the family sees about itself and wants formally to continue. It seems essential for an understanding of family life that we study this: it may be highly important for the happiness of the family that we seek to encourage and promote it. Kimball Young once referred to ritual as the core and essence of culture patterns;[3] we are emphasizing family ritual as the heart of family culture patterns.

Family Accord, Fixation, and the Process of Regression

As we passed from one family to another, studying the particular rituals of each, we came to think more and more of the problems of the persons who passed from the rituals of one family to those of another, not as students, but as members of these families. Persons frequently pass from one family and its rituals to another, and in various ways. The most obvious way is to leave the parental roof and form a new family. Cer-

[2] For an elaboration of this threefold conception of the family and other social institutions, see James H. S. Bossard, *The Sociology of Child Development*, New York, Harper & Brothers, 1948, chapters II-VI; and James H. S. Bossard and Eleanor S. Boll, *Family Situations*, Philadelphia, University of Pennsylvania Press, 1943, chapters I-V.

[3] Kimball Young, *Social Psychology*, New York, Alfred A. Knopf, Inc., 1930, p. 29.

tain aspects of this in regard to ritual changes were discussed in Chapter 8. But a substantial proportion of marriages are remarriages, for one or both marital partners who may or may not have children from the previous marriage. In such cases, the parent comes from the parental home previously established to found still another one. The children must adjust to changes in ritualistic observances at an earlier age. Then there are other transfers from one family to another—the widow who goes to live with a sister, son, or stranger; the family boarder who moves to another family; the house servant who changes employers; the orphan child who goes to a foster home or institution. What is the importance of the ritualistic readjustments that changes from one home to another involves?

We have become particularly involved in the meaning of differences in attitudes toward ritual for marital relations. Over and over again, in the course of this study, we noticed that married adults referred to such differences in attitudes between husband and wife. These comments came both from our cases and from adults with whom the study was discussed from time to time. In some instances they were mentioned as mere differences of opinion as to what seemed important or not in family living; at other times, the references seemed to imply that such differences were important for domestic relations. Not that failure to agree on family rituals was ever mentioned as a cause for a knockdown and drag-out family fight. Usually the references were rueful or wistful: "My wife, she doesn't care much for such things." "I miss that in my husband." "We were brought up differently at our house."

Partly evident are these differences in attitude toward ritual in inter-class marriages. We have long considered an analysis of the role of class differences in marriage a vital necessity in our family literature, and our case material further substantiates this point of view. We cite here one of our cases bearing on this point, given to us by a school friend of the woman:

She, Laura, was a girl, who, though of the same family background and economic status as the rest of us, had lost her mother when she was a baby, and had been brought up by a housekeeper who was hired by Laura's father during the daze which followed his wife's death, and which never left him as long as he lived. I knew this "dame" well. She was the hired housekeeper type, who has as her only aim, marriage to the man of the house, but who never made the grade, chiefly because he lived in a perpetual daze. She never made the slightest attempt to integrate the family. She only did the necessary chores in order to keep her job; and concentrated upon the Mr. There just were no family rituals. Home was a place to get out of. But Laura, of course, was sent to a private school along with the rest of us, though her home life was very different. She was a sweet and appealing girl. We liked and felt sorry for her, and she was intrigued with us and with our homes. During high school years, she just about put herself in the hands of the happy ten who formed our clique, and would not even buy clothes unless one of us went with her. We thought we were pretty smart, because Laura's looks improved. We also got dates for her from our own circle of friends, because we did not like the kind of boys she went with. She loved the manners of these boyfriends of ours, and set them up as an ideal. But she was nevertheless more popular with boys of a different sort. Well . . . after college, she had an affair with a man of the kind she aspired to. She got pregnant, and he was very chivalrous and "eloped" with her. She lost the baby. It was about six months after this that she came to talk to me. From my diary, I got her firsthand comments. For Bill, her husband, there was a way to do everything. Every Sunday, they had to spend at his parents' home, "Being stuffy" (having high tea). She had to keep a book of dates in which to remember the anniversaries of his whole family and send appropriate gifts; every holiday was a "commotion," when they had to do certain things and spend the day with certain of his relatives; if she happened to be out late in the afternoon and put table mats hurriedly on the dinner table instead of a cloth, Bill would say, "Is this breakfast or dinner?" In spite of the fact that their physical relationship was ideal, so she said, she felt she couldn't stand this way of living any longer. She felt "stifled." I didn't know what it was all about, and was of no help whatsoever. Very shortly, they got a divorce, though Bill also came over to talk to Frank and me. He adored Laura, and he, too, didn't know what it was all about. I remember that at the time we three all wondered if Laura had not been made a neuro-psychiatric case, because of the loss of her baby! Anyway, two years later, Laura married an Austrian Jew, who, in his desire to become American, had broken off with his family completely. I know him well, and like him, but know very little about his home life except that he has sloughed it off. The two of them lead the darnedest life, according to the standards of the ten of us who were high school classmates; and they are a constant subject of humorous comment. They never do anything according to Hoyle, and their life is very strange and completely haphazard. But the fact is that they are completely happy, and have been, since 1939. At the moment, and at their late age, they are thinking about adopting a couple of babies. My friends think the idea repulsive. I'm not so sure.

In seeking to assess the role of ritualistic background in child and youth development, and its subsequent role in marital relations, one inevitably is led to think of the processes of fixation and regression which have become so fundamental in the study of behavior.

The psychoanalysts seem to think of these two processes as part of their special contributions, and the idea of fixation is, of course, basic to the whole Freudian approach to the study of behavior, for it is the kind of thinking which implies that present manifestations are not only conditioned by the past, but contain nothing but the past. One is reminded here of Freud's concept of the timelessness of the unconscious, meaning that fears, desires, or even entire experiences which are repressed in childhood, although uninfluenced by further experience, because of their repression, remain nevertheless unaltered in their intensity and specific quality.[4]

A fixation, as the term is used by psychoanalysts, may be thought of, then, as a persistent and excessive unconscious wish for a specific form of earlier experience. As such, it may pertain not only to a certain person in the early environment, but may concern also a whole stage of libido development. No stage of life or experience in life is thus ever left behind or forgotten. A certain amount of libido continues to attach to every earlier phase of organization: it is fixated.

The existence of these fixations in the individual predisposes him to what is termed "regression." This is defined as the process whereby the individual attempts to obtain grati-

[4] Karen Horney, *New Ways in Psychoanalysis*, New York, W. W. Norton & Company, 1939, Chapter VIII.

fication in a way he found satisfactory when he was younger, that is, an attempt at adjustment through a backward movement along the channels of earlier infantile habits.

Without questioning the importance of the psychoanalysts in the development of these concepts, it might be pointed out that William James had much the same idea in speaking of the inhibition of instincts by habit:

When objects of a certain class elicit from an animal a certain sort of reaction, it often happens that the animal becomes partial to the first specimen of the class on which it has reacted, and will not afterwards react to another specimen.

The selection of a particular hole to live in, of a particular mate, of a particular feeding ground, a particular variety of diet, a particular anything, in short, out of a possible multitude, is a very widespread tendency among animals, even those low down in the scale. The limpet will return to the same sticking place in its rock, and the lobster to its favorite nook on the sea-bottom. The rabbit will deposit its dung in the same corner; the bird makes its nest on the same bough. But each of these performances carries with it an insensibility to other opportunities and occasions—an insensibility which can only be described physiologically as an inhibition of the new impulses by the habit of the old ones already formed. . . . A habit, once grafted on an instinctive tendency, restricts the range of the tendency itself, and keeps us from reacting on any but the habitual object, although other objects might just as well have been chosen had they been the first-comers.[5]

Wresting the general idea from the foregoing contexts, it would seem that we are dealing with a very general process that can be expressed quite simply as follows: *The normal individual, in his passage through the various stages of his social development, shows strong attachment to experiences and situations in earlier stages of that development, the strength of such attachment varying with the satisfactory nature of that experience or situation.* This would seem to be the essence of fixation and regression, in their larger aspects; of homesickness; of the nostalgic complex which evidences itself in a wide variety of ways.

[5] William James, *Principles of Psychology,* Volume II, p. 394.

Thus conceived, fixation may occur at any stage of development, as for instance at the adolescent level, with the acceptance of adolescent forms of behavior as adequate means of satisfaction and achievement. This is particularly apt to happen today, with what John Fiske called the prolongation of infancy, such as one finds in the case of college students. Blos has touched briefly upon this. Young people going to college cannot engage in many of the experiments in living that are normal accompaniments of adolescence, cannot achieve emancipation from their families, cannot obtain jobs, cannot establish families. Life takes the form of a protracted adolescence, and a fixation of social behavior as well as the conception of the self occurs at that level.[6] Surely everyone familiar with institutions of higher learning has seen these cases of arrested development, clinging after their graduation to the college, the fraternity house, the athletic field, etc., unwilling to venture into the paths of adult competition or withdrawing after brief unsuccessful forays into them.

This fixation of patterns of behavior is a very common occurrence. There is no justification for decorating it with the verbiage, and making it the property of any professional group. Its essence is the retention of patterns of behavior and situations fixed in earlier stages of development and the effort, often insistent, to maintain them in later stages even under quite differing circumstances. As such it is a recurring social process, the key explanation to many crises in the lives of individuals. It explains the worker who expects to be treated as when he was a child, the wife who wants to remain a spoiled daughter, the student who cries when given a low grade, or the man who marries a woman older than himself.

Certainly these concepts throw light on much of the material gathered in this study. The basic facts in our thinking in this area of the study may be summarized briefly:

1. Many, perhaps most, family rituals develop with the coming of children. Often they partake of the nature of a family

6 Peter Blos, *The Adolescent Personality*, New York, D. Appleton-Century Company, 1941, p. 325.

drama, designed to impress the children. Many rituals center about the children; usually they participate in them.

2. Many family rituals cannot but make a vivid impression upon children. Proof of this constantly appeared as the study progressed—in the clarity of the recollection, the willingness to coöperate in the study, the pride in pointing out the details and features of the rituals, displayed by younger persons interviewed by us. Here again we recall the tendency of the authors of autobiographies to view their early family life in terms of recurring family rituals.

3. Many, even if not all, of the family rituals recalled, have pleasant associations. Often they center about holidays, birthdays, anniversaries, and other happy occasions. Because of the nature of family rituals—their recurrence, the sense of rightness which accompanies them, the pleasurable associations—they groove themselves deeply and pleasantly into the accumulating layers of the youthful mind, which constitutes the essence of the unconscious.

4. When the individual leaves home, a major part of the readjustment involves the change in ritualistic behavior. Marriage and the formation of a new family is such an occasion, obviously. Both mates bring their respective experiences with family rituals with them to form the new family. Similarity in such experiences seems to be an important factor in making for marital success; lack of it appears to have the opposite effect.

5. When one's experience with family ritual has been a happy one, fixation may occur. Later on, although one has left home and even formed his or her own family, there is the insistent longing for the earlier experience to be repeated. It is at this point that one begins to understand the many remarks made to us about the lack of interest in family ritual of the matrimonial mate. Now, too, the wife who insists that she, her husband, and the children, return to her parents' home on various occasions. Apparent, too, is the behavior of the husband or wife who returns periodically for protracted visits to the parents' home. Focusing on ritualistic background, we are now in a position to understand why Jane, married but

two years, finds her in-laws so difficult. She has been accustomed to a ritualized family life: they have not. Or why Bill finds Hester so matter of fact and the home she makes for him so colorless and lifeless.

Family Ritual and Family Integration

"The family," writes Burgess and Locke, "like all organisms, is in a process of constant accommodation to environing and to internal forces. Perhaps more than any other social group, it is a demonstration or an experiment in the integration of heterogeneous elements; heterogeneous in age, sex and temperament, and often also in social experience, economic activities, and cultural background."[7]

Perhaps the overall conclusion that emerges from the assemblage of our material is that ritual is a relatively reliable index of family integration. What do we mean by family integration? Does it mean absence of discord? Obviously this is an aspect or index of it, even if negative in character. Is it ability to withstand shock or stress or strain? Possibly, but this would seem to be somewhat a matter of accepted values, and character traits of the constituent members rather than an interactive product or structural strength. The word "integrate" means to bring together and to make into a whole, and we use the term "family integration" to mean the welding or unification of its diverse elements into a complex whole or harmonious relationship. An integrated family means to us a well-knit family, one bound together with strong and continuing ties, and functioning smoothly as a unit.

If one conceives of family integration in generic terms, there are many indexes which may be utilized to identify it. These include the effective meeting of common problems, the ability to resist major crises, smoothness of operation, lack of tension or conflict, evidences of family pride, criteria of family coöperation and continuity, and continuity of family planning. Thinking in terms of process, family integration is unrelated to moral

[7] Ernest W. Burgess and Harvey J. Locke, *The Family*, New York, The American Book Company, 1945, p. 579.

purposes or cultural values. A well-integrated family may evidence it in recurrent feuding with another family, in packing boxes for shipment to displaced persons, in periodic outbursts of drunkenness, or long-range planning for the successive education of the children in a large family.

Ritual indicates many things and serves many purposes in the life of a family. The existence of well-established ritual implies, for example, a considerable amount of likemindedness among the members of a family. Take such a simple yet basic fact as a common interest in family life. The development of a ritual by a family is an index of the common interest of its members in the family as a group. Parents who are conscious of the family as a group, who wish to make a success of family living, who think of their family as a continuing and permanent arrangement, are the ones most likely to initiate and continue the coöperative procedure which yields as a ritual. One can detect, therefore, at the very beginning, a selective process between those family members who develop and utilize ritual, and those who do not. One must be interested in his family, want to make a go of it, and think of it as a permanent relationship, to look forward to the establishment of family rituals and traditions.

Again, rituals are developed coöperatively. This gives and stimulates a sense of group participation, a further sharing of intimacies, and a sense of lively satisfaction. As Adams pointed out years ago, the feelings of satisfaction that accompany the performance of ritual, and the "pause of satisfaction" that follows the achievement of ends in mind, constitute the essence of the aesthetic experience. In other words, the aesthetic experience is a concomitant of successful participation in the ritualistic act.[8] "The rite is performed; control is achieved; the participants rest satisfied."[9]

Third, common participation is a ceremony that carries with it a sense of rightness that makes for family pride. One senses

---

[8] Elizabeth Kemper Adams, *The Aesthetic Experience*, Chicago, University of Chicago Press, 1907.

[9] Henke, *op. cit.*, p. 84.

this feeling of pride in almost all of our case records. Even if there was a sort of playful apology, or grumbling pose of feminine coyness in the lines of the case record, it was easy to detect the shades of smug satisfaction between the lines which described the family rituals. The eager willingness with which so many persons coöperated in this study has already been mentioned. Apparently family pride makes for ritual, ritual makes for family pride.

Next, many of our rituals involve refinements of living, and adherence to them implies, and stimulates, a common interest in such refinements. Ritual necessitates a certain formality in social relations, and complementary to this are consideration for the rights of others and the discipline of self, all of which makes for good group relations. It is obvious from our material that ritualism and formalism in family relations make for predictability of behavior response, and this tends to reduce strain and disorder.

The limitations of space permit the mention of but one other role of ritual in family life, and that is its frequent service as a means of controlling the behavior of its members. L. L. Bernard speaks of this aspect of ritual in his *Social Control*,[10] and we have found many instances of this role in our material. Most of our cases have to do with its use to control the behavior of younger members of the household, to regiment and standardize their conduct. Some technique proves to be successful, always produces the same result, and thus comes to be ritualized. But not all cases deal with the control of children. Mother is not above the utilization of ritual to regiment a not completely reliable husband, and at least one husband and his children, in view of Mother's immunity to the inexorableness of the clock, copy a page from the late King Edward VII whenever the family is invited to any occasion. (Edward VII had all clocks in his home set one hour ahead, to enable him more nearly to meet engagements on scheduled time.)

In emphasizing ritual as a significant index of family inte-

[10] L. L. Bernard, *Social Control*, The Macmillan Co., 1939, p. 434.

gration and conserver of family values, we run a certain risk of being misunderstood. Some cynical soul, in looking over our detailed material, might notice, for example, a ritual in which the entire family gather nightly to drink grape juice before retiring, and rush to interpret us to say: "Drink grape juice before going to bed and have a happy family life." Some of the criticism of the Burgess-Cortrell study comes very close to being of this sort.

This, however, is far from the point we wish to emphasize here. The evening drink and the grape juice are wholly incidental and trivial. What is significant is that the family gathers nightly, engages in a common experience, relaxes together, and exchanges comments before retiring. In thus participating in a recurrent event, which involves some degree of coöperation, the members of the family promote their common life and group rapport. One final word of anticipatory defense. For every conclusion presented, there is case material to support and illustrate it. But for virtually each of our findings, there are also contrary cases. Just as there are speculators who play the stock market on the theory of *Contrary Opinion*, i.e., bucking the majority trends, so there are persons and families who behave "the other way." We not only admit these cases, but we are trying also to understand them. The exception as well as the rule is grist for the mills of the scientists, and the gods as well.

Basically, what we have been trying to show is that ritualizing is a process of family interaction and culture transmission, and that its role depends upon its content and the manner of its utilization. A ritual, appealing in content and manipulated wisely, becomes a powerful and constructive weapon in the integration of a family; and an ill-adapted ritual or a good ritual misused may become an agent in its disintegration. This, perhaps, will serve to explain both our generalizations and the exceptions to them.

Summary

1. A recapitulation of earlier emphases shows that writers of autobiographies largely picture their childhood family ex-

periences in terms of family rituals; that the comments of university students emphasize rituals as easing stress and strain in group living as well as serving to condition the behavior of younger family members; that rituals are an integral part of the family culture varying definitely from one class level to another; and that while the rituals of a family vary from one stage of its development to another, some persist through the years from one generation to another.

2. Rituals regularize personal relations, both of the family as a whole, and between individual members. Particularly significant is the regularization of relations between husband and wife, and parent and child.

3. Ritual is suggested as the best starting point for the study of family culture patterns. Family rituals are the core of the family culture.

4. Passage from the life in one family to that in another calls for ritualistic readjustments. Marriage brings together persons of different ritualistic backgrounds. Earlier family experiences with rituals may result in fixations and resultant regressions in the subject married life of the individual.

5. The overall conclusion that emerges from the assemblage of our material is that ritual is a relatively reliable index of family integration.

6. Exceptions to the conclusions presented in this volume are admitted freely, and supported by case material. These exceptions are recognized as fruitful leads for further study.

10

The Study of Family Life: A Methodological Postscript

The conceptions with which sociological science is concerned, are complex beyond all others. In the absence of faculty having a corresponding complexity, they cannot be grasped. Here, however, as in other cases, the absence of an adequately complex faculty is not accompanied by any consciousness of incapacity. Rather do we find that deficiency in the required kind of mental grasp is accompanied by extreme confidence of judgment on sociological questions, and a ridicule of those who, after long discipline, begin to perceive what there is to be understood, and how difficult is the right understanding of it.[1]

IN THESE words Herbert Spencer, writing in the third quarter of the nineteenth century, laid his fingers on what he considered one of the major difficulties in the study of sociology. The volume from which this passage is quoted remains, despite the passing years, almost the only frank, comprehensive assessment of the difficulties, objective and subjective, which inhere in the development of a social science.

Perhaps no reputable sociologist would deny the reality of this difficulty, nor the fact that the failure to recognize this

[1] Herbert Spencer, *The Study of Sociology*, New York and London, D. Appleton and Company, 1873, p. 115.

complexity is manifest in some sociological work and writing down to the present time. Obviously it expresses itself in numerous ways—the over-simplification of problems; the failure to appreciate the interrelatedness of social phenomena; the misunderstandings and quarrels between differing and contending approaches to sociological data, each assuming itself to be the only correct one, to mention but some of the more apparent instances.

More and more, however, sociologists have come to recognize the scope and complexity of the field within which they work, the myriad facets of it to be explored, the necessity for many differing approaches, the inevitability of conflicting yet complementary points of view, and the interrelationship between their own specialized tasks and those in other social sciences. All this has made for mutual toleration and respect of each others' work. By common consent of gentlemen's agreement, sociologists today tend less and less to snipe at the propriety or orthodoxy of each other's work, counseling only on the soundness of their respective conclusions and procedures, as each meanwhile digs in at some promising place in the rich hinterland to be exploited.

Approaches to the Study of the Family

The family is society in miniature. There is perhaps no problem or principle of human relationships which cannot be found within the confines of a large household. As Quintilian, the famous Roman rhetorician of the "Silver Age," once remarked: "For exploring human nature, one household is large enough." From this it follows that all that has been said about the complexity of sociological data may be said with equal propriety about the study of the human family. Family life is richly complex. It is important always to remember this if the field of the family is to be fully explored. Similarly, the family needs to be studied from many points of view; there are many facets to be considered, each with its own appropriate methodology, and in relation to the larger whole of its reality.

A brief review of the sociological literature on the family

will serve to identify some of the approaches which have been made thus far in its scientific study. One might almost think of the basic implications of these approaches as so many dimensions of family life, and the work that has been done on each as efforts to measure the family in terms of these dimensions.

One common approach regards the family primarily as an aspect or echo of the larger society, The family, in other words, is a funnel or bottleneck through which flows the everyday life of society. Thus conceived, the main concern and problems considered become those which deal with the impact of society upon the family. How does the prevailing system of economic production and distribution affect the family? What do social changes, social crises, and social catastrophes mean for family life? What is the significance of mechanical invention? Of revolutionary changes in prevailing ideologies, such as those which result from modern science? What is the meaning of war for relations between husband and wife, and parent and child? How do revolutionary changes in popular transportation media, or in patterns of population distribution, come to be assimilated into the family pattern? Here, in other words, is that plethora of interrelations between a large assortment of social forces on the one hand and, on the other, such basic matters as family forms, functions, size, structure, and the like.

Another, and somewhat contrasting approach, emphasizes the family as a psychosocial group, in which go on constantly the interactive processes which constitute the essence of life of its members and serve so largely to condition their respective personalities. The basic emphases here are upon the personalities of the members of the family, and what they do to each other in the incisive and intimate exchange of family relationships. How does the family operate, directly and indirectly, obviously and adroitly, to control and to influence the behavior of its members?

Then there is the approach which conceives of the family primarily in terms of adult relationships, principally those between husband and wife. The emphasis now shifts to such problems as mate selection, marriage procedures, and adjustment within marriage as expressed in terms of happiness, unhappiness, overt discord, family disorganization, and ultimate disintegration. Marriage is the culmination of the romantic attachment of two persons to each other, its purpose is their mutual happiness, its success is measured by the continuity of such a relationship. Problems such as these accord with the romantic interests of the members of college and university classes for whose use so much of the current literature on the family is developed, and as a result, more attention has been given to this aspect of family life than any other.

Still other systematic studies of the family focus attention upon its fundamental recurrent function, i.e., as the basic social relationship between successive generations. Societal continuity is contingent upon family continuity and, in many ways, all other aspects of family life are incidental to its two main historical purposes: one, the biological function of physical reproduction; and second, the transmission of the cultural stream to the next generation. Stripped of all other sources, the human family is a device of nature to continue the race biologically and culturally. Thus considered, problems of the birth rate and infant mortality, the processes of child rearing, education, child guidance, and the care of aged members, are assigned major importance.

Finally, the family may be studied as a social institution, in terms of historical growth and changes. This historical approach, which characterized a good deal of the earlier work on the family, is in keeping with the evolutionary emphasis in modern science. In studies of this kind, the family is surveyed in the retrospect of time—the extended family of the Chinese, the patriarchial form among the Romans, the family in an agricultural regime, the American colonial type, and that of our contemporary urban culture. Consideration is given in these cases to the forms and functions of the family as weighed in the balance of historical experience, as well as to the processes whereby family structures and procedures are adapted to the stage setting of the larger society, and affect it also in turn.

Just as each of the foregoing approaches to the study of the family has its own distinctive purpose and value, so each has been developed on the basis of its own appropriate methodology.Relationships between family and society, involving mass phenomena, come to rely heavily, even if not wholly, upon quantitative methods. Similar is the reliance in a consideration of problems of the birth rate, infant mortality, desertion, divorce, and the like. On the other hand, when the approach is historical and interpretative in terms of social process, the primary methodological need comes to be that of evaluating sources and bodies of historical evidence. Finally, when the problems studied fall within the field of family interaction, and particularly within its more subtle processes, still other tools and methods must be utilized. The operation of ritual, for example, like the processes of family table talk, family entertainment, and word usages, which were subjects of our earlier studies, elude for the most part the straitjacket of the questionnaire method, the naïveté of a statistical table, or the balance sheet of a social accounting system. It seems proper therefore to turn at this point to an examination of the sources of information utilizied, and some of the techniques emphasized, in this study.

Source Materials for the Present Study

The study of family ritual presented in this volume is an original one, based on some four hundred case records. These were obtained from six sources: authors of autobiographies, university students, residents surrounding a social settlement and participating in its activities, residents in a middle-class suburban area, members of the Junior League, and a number of unselected adults who agreed to participate in the study. In some of the cases, the material is self-recorded (seventy-three autobiographical accounts and eighty-six university student essays): in other cases, questionnaires were distributed to persons to whom the project was explained and who agreed to coöperate; in still other instances, interactive interviews with individuals and families were recorded. Forty case records were built up at considerable length by this latter method, and it was also used to supplement and verify material gathered by questionnaires and free associational writing. Supplementing many of the case records, and particularly those obtained from the interactive interviews, were observations made by us and recorded over a period of time without the knowledge of the individuals and families concerned.

Some further reference to the value of some of the sources of our information would seem to be in order. To begin with, a considerable proportion of our material consists of descriptions of family rituals, furnished by university students in the form of free associational writing. How valuable are students as sources of such information? Several considerations bearing on this question present themselves. First, university students are a relatively intelligent group, with high capacity to grasp exposition, covering both the project as a whole and their own part in it. Second, they have the ability to verbalize and to express social facts. This is a significant factor in research into human behavior, and the more one seeks to secure information from people, the more does one come to be impressed with its importance. Again, the continuing relations between students and instructor are such that the relative reliability of information given may be judged, details of it may be verified, and confusions may be dispelled. Then, too, interest in a given research project may be aroused, so that coöperation again becomes active, eager, alert, and continuing. In our own case, we have sought to stimulate student coöperation by allowing academic credit for equivalent work done; and we have sought to allow for sufficient time to permit the play of mental association to follow its meandering way. Finally, university students are at an age customarily, when there exists a certain objectivity in their attitudes toward their respective families. They are in process of growing out of their families; in many cases they are living away from their families at the time; yet they remain as parts of them for the time being. It is our contention that in all of these respects university students compare very favorably as sources of evidence with natives in primitive cultures upon whom anthropologists must rely so heavily, or with sections of the general public that are utilized in all kinds of other studies of social behavior. To the reader's obvious reaction at this point that university students are heavily weighted on class and other bases, the equally obvious answer is that the problem of statistical sampling prevails in any extended study, and that its particular importance in any given study depends upon the subject studied, and the conclusions drawn. In a pioneer study of ritual in family living a beginning must be made somewhere; the class and other variables are a matter of subsequent determination.

A second important source of our material consists of descriptions of family rituals found in published autobiographies, and it seems partinent here to refer to the development of autobiographical material and assess briefly its value for the purposes to which we have utilized it.

Ever since there has been a reading public of any size, biography has ranked next to fiction in popularity, and most readers of biography would agree with what Dr. Johnson wrote in 1759:

> Those relations are therefore commonly of most value in which the writer tells his own story. . . . The writer of his own life has at least the first qualification of an historian, the knowledge of the truth; and although it may be plausibly objected that his temptations to disguise it are equal to his opportunities of knowing it, yet I cannot but think that impartiality may be expected with equal confidence from him that relates the passages of his own life, as from him that delivers the transactions of another. . . . He that speaks of himself has no motive to falsehood or partiality except self-love, by which all have so often been betrayed that we are on the watch against its artifices.[2]

The word "autobiography" was coined by Robert Southey in 1809, and in the years since, during which time it has attained eminent respectability as a type of literature, two major forms of autobiography have developed. In the one form, the emphasis is largely or wholly upon the external events in the author's life, and he regards these as important primarily because they

[2] Quoted from Richard D. Mallery, *Masterworks of Autobiography*, New York, Doubleday & Company, 1946, p. 3.

have occurred during memorable days and in relation to larger events which he wishes to discuss. The second form deals chiefly with inner events, in which the author directs attention to himself and his personal development, and in which he is concerned principally with describing his own thoughts and feelings. Although most autobiographies combine aspects of both forms, one can perhaps agree with the statement that "what we call the great autobiographies have almost without exception been records of inner experience rather than of outward events."[3]

Autobiographical material seems particularly pertinent in the study of family and child life because the autobiographer so frequently writes with considerable minuteness of his childhood and youth. Much of the fascination of this kind of literature, it has been pointed out, comes from the opportunity it gives us to observe great men as children.

We watch with interest Saint Augustine disliking school and having trouble with the Greek language; Cellini taking music lessons only to please his father; Rousseau showing no promise whatsoever, much to the despair of his relatives; Goethe visiting art galleries instead of attending law lectures; Franklin planning to run away; Tolstoy failing to pass his examinations and utterly unable to get along with his tutor; Newman reading the *Arabian Nights* and wishing they were true; Andersen playing with his puppet theater; young Henry Adams serenely confident that he would one day be President.[4]

The values and defects of autobiographies in the study of behavior have been discussed by Allport, Krueger, Burr, Murchison, and others.[5] Reference is made to the fact that recollections recorded in autobiographies do not as a rule extend into that very early period of life which today is con-

[3] *Ibid.*, p. 5.
[4] *Ibid.*, p. 8.
[5] Gordon W. Allport, *The Use of Personal Documents in Psychological Science*, New York, Social Science Research Council, 1942. See also Louis Gottschalk, Clyde Kluckholm, and Robert Angell, *The Use of Personal Documents in History, Anthropology, and Sociology*, New York, Social Science Research Council, 1945.

sidered so significant for its formative functions, as well as other aspects of unreliability. By way of contrasting emphasis, certain values of autobiographical material, noted elsewhere,[6] may be recapitulated here. First, material presented in auto-biographies comes without reference to the promptings and suggestions of any research project. The research worker who subsequently goes to an autobiography for data relating to his project finds information that is both objective and spontaneous. Second, autobiographers, even more than students, usually have some experience and facility in expressing their ideas. They write well and verbalize readily—at least in comparison with persons from whom so much of the material bearing upon behavior problems has been obtained. Furthermore, they have had some experience in thinking through the processes of human development, even if only their own, and in express-ing them in effective form and manner. Obviously the effort to write a readable autobiography involves the possible defects resulting from striving for effective expression, possibly at the risk of complete truthfulness. In writing human material, there is often the temptation to add "the fictional touch." Possibly this would be less true in recalling childhood family experiences than in certain other areas of life. Finally, it should be noted that in writing about family rituals, many of the defects imputed to autobiographical writing would not apply. Family ritual is nothing that autobiographers, or students, would hesitate to tell or write about. Family ritual would be in most cases a matter of pride rather than the focus of inhibitions which would limit the amount or nature of self-revelation.

Turning to a third source, particular reliance has been placed by us upon the more extended case histories, built up through interactive interviews and continued often over a consider-able period of time. In these cases we sought to build up a complete understanding of, and continuing interest in, the study as a whole. Every effort was made to explain the con-cept of family ritual, the nature of the study, and the kinds

[6] James H. S. Bossard, *The Sociology of Child Development*, New York, Harper & Brothers, 1948, pp. 238-239.

of material obtained from other sources. Our coöperating personnel were encouraged then to describe rituals, past and present, in their own family backgrounds. In some cases they were encouraged to write out an original draft, which was then discussed with them; in a majority of these cases, however, all of the material was obtained orally. Most frequently, such persons would return more than once for interviews, often at their own suggestion. In virtually all of the forty lengthy case histories, the final record represented an accumulation of material built up over a period of weeks and months, rather than of one lengthy interview.

Some Techniques in Family Study

In the gathering of information through personal interviews three techniques have been assiduously cultivated. The first is that of *inconspicuous listening*. The importance of this is manifest, but an emphasis upon it seems necessary in a world in which "nobody wants to listen and everyone wants to talk." This brash inclination is not confined to professional commentators and cocktail habitués. The senior author encountered it unexpectedly, years ago, among scientists. After devoting two years to a study of the problems of university education for business,[7] he was invited upon a number of occasions by scientifically trained persons to tell informally the substance of his findings. With but few exceptions, such conversations became, after a few minutes, a recital by the questioner of what the questionee had really discovered. That is to say, he was told what he had discovered in the course of his research.

To listen, and to do so sympathetically and helpfully, is not merely good manners but is an important asset in the investigation of human behavior. Also, it is an art. The historic church made it a sacrament. Psychiatrists, psychologists, psychoanalysts, and social workers have emphasized it. Social scientists have not paid much attention to it; many of them are poor listeners. Their professional drives and training are directed

[7] James H. S. Bossard and J. Frederic Dewhurst, *University Education for Business,* Philadelphia, University of Pennsylvania Press, 1931.

toward talking. Especially may lecturing predispose against good listening. From "telling them" habitually to listening patiently and effectively is a difficult transition.

Dr. Carl Rogers has rendered recently a distinctive service in emphasizing the use of the "nondirective method" for social research.[8] He sees the most promising use of this technique in the realm of personality research, and as a corrective against the aggressive tendency of asking questions. "We have noted in clinical work," he writes, "that, after several client-centered interviews, the dynamics of personality development and adjustment are much more clearly brought out than in a wealth of factual material gained through questions."[9]

More recently, Russell L. Dicks, writing out of a background of pastoral work, has treated suggestively this art of listening. He differentiates between several kinds of listening. One kind, *directive listening*, utilizes questions by the listener. It is a common but rather dangerous method, according to Dicks, having the disadvantage of aggressiveness, and unless used adroitly, defeating its own purposes. *Supportive listening* is another kind. It may be called passive listening, for it involves comparative passiveness of the listener as he emotionally supports the other person while he unfolds his story. Among other things, this means being alert, nodding your head encouragingly, looking at the speaker and then away, waiting patiently as he talks, relaxing within your own body so as not to block or resist what is being said, and above all little grunts of *ah* and *um* and *um huh*.[10]

The preceding distinctions seem to give added emphasis to our concept of *inconspicuous listening* as a process in the study of family behavior in which the investigator absorbs information without an awareness of the process on the part of those studied. Obviously, such unawareness can never be quite complete with the presence of a non-member in the family circle; by

[8] Carl R. Rogers, "The Nondirective Method as a Technique for Social Research," *The American Journal of Sociology*, January, 1945, pp. 279-83.

[9] *Ibid.*, p. 281.

[10] Russell L. Dicks, "The Pastor's Use of Creative Listening," *Mental Hygiene*, October, 1948, pp. 578-85.

conscious effort, one can, however, approximate it to a very considerable extent.

A second technique is that of *inconspicuous observation*, with reference primarily to two aspects of the family interactive process. One of these includes the observation of the overt activities of the persons in interaction. In other words, what do members of the family do in addition to what they say? Second are the non-symbolic forms of human communication, such as gestures, facial expressions, and the like. In part, these are an aspect of preverbal communication, such as parents use in their relations with younger children, but in larger measure, and especially so far as our present interest is concerned, they are physical expressions of emotions. As such they serve many functions—the identification of underlying tensions, the addition of expressive overtones, and the modification of verbal statements. The facial expression may give the lie to the spoken word, or it may underscore it. Tension in the body posture may contradict the cordial expression of interest, and rapt attention may be more eloquent than the spoken word. And here again obvious observation introduces a sense of awareness which may defeat its own purpose. The more one can see without the appearance of noticing, the more valuable is the observation.

One cannot but recall here the emphasis upon observation given by Cannon in his discussion of the fitness of the investigator for his task. Writing out of his own background in medical research, he says;

The investigator should not only possess but also train himself in keen powers of observation. He should be alert asd watchful as events transpire in the course of experiments, so that nothing escapes his vigilance. We readily behold the familiar; we may overlook the unfamiliar. An old saying has it: "We are prone to see what lies behind our eyes rather than what appears before them."[11]

It goes without saying that if this be true in the study of microbes it would seem to have some importance in the study of family behavior.

[11] Walter B. Cannon, *The Way of An Investigator*, W. W. Norton & Company, 1945, p. 36.

A third technique is that of *unsuspected recording*, by which we mean putting down in written form everything we can of what we have heard and seen. We have no hestitation in saying that any awareness of a written record of the behavior of the family studied introduces immediately elements of artificiality that tend to destroy the value of the study. One has noticed this even in the giving of a medical history to an elderly and trusted physician.

Coupled with this is the need for complete recording. In more ways than one, nothing that has been noted should be overlooked, however trivial it may seem. An excellent example comes to hand as this is being written. In a series of entries in a case record kept in the files of the William T. Carter Foundation and accumulating since June 1947, an incidental fact, at first not recorded as being too trivial, but finally included under date of November 10, 1947, furnishes the key to events which took place in May 1948.

The reader will combine at once two requirements. That records be kept without the knowledge of the family studied, and that they be as complete as possible; and he will be tempted to say: "It's a good trick if one can manage it." Obviously this is true and it must be admitted that these two ends can be achieved only partially. Several helpful aids, however, may be suggested. One, of course, is the use of an automatic recording device. There are certain circumstances under which their use is feasible and permissible. Again, there are times when the help of members of families, who have experience in shorthand recording, can be utilized. Also, a great deal can be done by memory recording. If one sets himself to this task, it is remarkable how much of an activity and attendant conversation may be faithfully recorded. "A retentive and facile memory is a highly important qualification," writes Cannon in assessing the requisite requirements for fitness for scientific research.[12] One need only recall here the remarkable feats of memory constantly performed by theatrical performers who often memorize pages of lines upon a single hearing or reading.

[12] *Ibid.*, p. 36.

Complete recording of behavior, and especially of conversation, involves an excursion into the realities of life. To record verbatim a conversation between several persons is an intriguing experience; to read one's own participation in it may be a devastating experience. The recording of conversation, it will be recalled, is the chief method utilized by the dramatist and novelist to portray character and it is not too much to say that Sinclair Lewis wrote his way earlier to a Nobel prize by recording faithfully the small talk of a small town and retailing it in fictional form. Truth is fiction, when it is accurately reported; or would it be more nearly correct to say that truth is stranger than fiction, particularly if it is spelled out in detail?

Adaptive Differentials in Methodology

One of the curious omissions in the literature on methodology in the study of human behavior is the relative failure to recognize the adaptations which need to be made (a) on the basis of the nature of the subject studied, and (b) of the differentials which exist among the people from whom the information is obtained. The common assumption seems to be that sound methodology is sound methodology, wherever and on whomever it is applied. Our experience in the study of the family is quite the reverse, emphasizing the fact that methodology is rather a relative matter which needs to be adapted, and re-adapted, constantly on the basis of circumstances encountered. One is reminded here of the experience of many novices when they turn to the game of golf. Instruction from golf mentors is apt to overwhelm the learner so completely with admonitions and rules on the "form" to be maintained that he forgets the main object of the game, which is to sink a golf ball in the next hole in the fewest possible number of strokes. It is not unlikely that many students of behavior are so overwhelmed with the emphasis on the technical forms and procedures in research that they forget the main object, which is to obtain new insight into a problem. All this, of course, is not said to depreciate the value of sound instruction and training in research: it is rather meant as a note of warning concerning a too slavish devotion to the relative emptiness of mere rule of thumb.

The first factor necessitating adaptions of methodology is the nature of the subject to be investigated. Consider, for example, such a difficult problem as sex behavior. What method or methods are of the greatest value in such a study? Kinsey and his associates[13] place their reliance on the personal interview, with much emphasis upon the methods of establishing contacts with cases; securing the interest, and self-interest, of those interviewed; the establishment of rapport between the interviewee and interviewer; and various technical devices in interviewing. By way of contrast, Lewis M. Terman, of no mean experience as an investigator of human behavior, suggests that some of the information sought by Kinsey and his associates "would have been more accurately reported had a method been used which prevented the investigator from learning the identity of any of his respondents."[14] Obviously, Terman has in mind the questionnaire method.

An example from our own experience might also be cited. For some years we have been seeking primary information on the child's discovery of the sex life of his parents. For many reasons, this is a painful and difficult subject on which to obtain data. Trial of various methods has led us to rely mainly on written accounts anonymously submitted. By explaining fully the nature of our quest to various groups of persons, we have sought, with limited success, to interest individuals in writing out a personal document in this field, with some accompanying but not specifically identifying information.

The study of family ritual has, by its very nature, been a relatively easy subject to study. There is nothing embarrassing about such a subject of investigation. Most families observe a few rituals, at least; most of them are quite willing, and often

[13] Alfred C. Kinsey, Wardell B. Pomeroy, and Clyde E. Martin, *Sexual Behavior in the Human Male*, Philadelphia, W. B. Saunders Company, 1948, Chapter II.

[14] Lewis M. Terman, "Kinsey's Sexual Behavior in the Human Male: Some Comments and Criticisms," *The Psychological Bulletin*, Volume 45, No. 5, September, 1948, p. 443.

eager, to tell or to write out accounts of them. The very sense or feeling of rightness which accompanies the observance of family rituals makes the informant willing to describe them ordinarily to the interested and sympathetic student. Our distinctive approach in this particular study, then, has been to assume with our cases that families ordinarily developed some rituals as a matter of course, that they were of all kinds and varieties, and that our main interest was in discovering their range and relative frequency. Other aspects and applications of the study were made known subsequently. This seemed on the whole a satisfactory mode of operation.

The second factor necessitating adaptions in the methodology of research into family behavior is to be found in the differences which prevail among the persons from whom information is obtained. Some persons are outgoing in their responses: frank, objective often, uninhibited to some degree at least. It is easy for them to look at their own behavior and to help you do so. There are others who are "tight-eared" or "tight-lipped," i.e., they have difficulty in understanding what it is that one wants to know, or in telling one if they do know. Differences of this kind are partly a matter of individual variation, but one comes also to wonder if there are not group differentials of this kind, as for instance between cultural groups. Do Jews as a group frequently combine introspective tendencies with willingness to verbalize to a relatively high degree? Is it true, as one has been told repeatedly, that the Pennsylvania German would rather "part with his right arm than tell his marital problems to anyone?" Does the reticence of the Vermonter carry over when he is a subject in a scientific investigation? Here is an intriguing problem in research methodology: to discover if, and to what extent, there are group differentials of this kind in responsiveness to social investigation, especially to questions and problems of a more personal and intimate kind?

Another striking difference between individuals, and groups, is to be found in their varying capacities to understand and use words. We have written elsewhere of the different levels of language at which families express themselves, and of the fact that social class marks the most striking line of cleavage in our language records of families.[15] These differences are of many kinds—words commonly used, use of imagery and figurative expressions, precision in word meaning, range of vocabulary and appreciation of verbal distinctions. One cannot consciously observe word usages among people without becoming aware of the fact that many persons do not verbalize readily, and hence have difficulty in understanding just what information is wanted, as well as in telling what they do know. These differences often coincide with educational and class levels. Certainly the use of the questionnaire, interview, or life history document must be guided to a large extent by the ability to verbalize of the individual or group involved. Here again is a challenging problem in research methods: How do social class differentials necessitate adaptions in research methodology?

Then there is the problem of the class status of the researcher in relation to that of the person from whom information is being sought. It is amazing that this problem has not been recognized in the literature of methodology. Whatever its role in the rote-gathering of certain kinds of objective data, its importance in the study of the intimate aspects of family living must be considerable. Certain aspects of this are obvious, even if their manifestations may be somewhat subtle. For example, upper-class families will give information of certain kinds only to upper-class seekers of that information. Middle-class families tend to withdraw if the interrogator is identified as of lower-class status. On the whole, class recognizes class and will speak of intimate matters only to social equals, or superiors. A feeling of kinship on the class level makes for rapport between a questioner and a questionee; awareness of class differences militate against it.

Similar to class differences is the role of ethnic differences. Feelings of discrimination on ethnic bases prevail widely among peoples the world over. Consciousness of kind, or lack of it, is a factor in research procedures, as well as in Gidding's

[15] James H. S. Bossard, *The Sociology of Child Development,* New York, Harper & Brothers, 1948, chapter IX.

interpretation of the social process. Lithuanians may hesitate to be frank about family matters with an Italian student; a Bulgarian family may "freeze up" against a Greek researcher; and an old New England family of Vermont persuasion may find it slightly difficult to speak freely of family matters to a Russian Jew. We are speaking here of psychological realities, not of professions of emotional evangelism, in the field of ethnic group relations.

Finally, to be noted here, is the attitude of the individual toward the particular subject of the research project. In the study of family ritual, we encountered a wide variation in personal attitude toward ritual. Some persons were frankly antagonistic, not necessarily to the study, but to the very idea of rituals in family living. The explanation of some of these cases inhered in the nature of their family situations and of the personalities involved, as for example, when a dominating parent imposes ritual upon a resistant child. Here the rebellion against the parent expresses itself also in rebellion against family ritual. In a few cases we found that, where the dominating parent was the mother and the rituals were mostly feminine in character, the rebellion was against the "sissiness" of the rituals. In most cases, however, such rejection is not personal but cultural, that is, the child rejects the culture of parents and kinfolk, as often happens in second generation immigrant families. In these cases, the child rejects the rituals in his family, and develops a skeptical or openly antagonistic attitude toward ceremonial aspects of his earlier life which are in any way associated with the family background which he rejects. One such case was Harold May. Harold is a Jew. His father is a scientist, who has no use for religion, or anything smacking of the ceremonial. The son is a scientist, too, realistic and "tough-minded." He has changed his name and is married to a gentile woman. A part of his life pattern involves a breaking away from Jewish connections, and one phase of this has been a rejection of all ceremonials of the Jewish group in particular and of the rituals in life in general. In contrast to such cases are those families, with a long and proud past in the prevailing culture, whose members are pleased to recall the rituals in their family experience, and who treasure them in later life.

On the whole, we are inclined to conclude that the attitude of a person toward ritual is a fairly reliable index of his integration into his background. Rebellion against family, church, or even school background seems to express itself in attitudes toward ritual, ranging from open antagonism to sly skepticism; friendly pride in ritual seems to betoken the acceptance of the group personnel and culture in which the ritual obtains.

The study of family ritual is a comparatively easy matter. It is a phase of the life of a family of which its members ordinarily are proud. Because of its very nature, there is a sense of rightness about it which predisposes family members to recall readily and to describe easily its nature, operation, and implications. There is less of a feeling of hesitation and shame about ritual than about most other phases of family life. One has the feeling, therefore, that family rituals, to which this volume is devoted, are as responsive to scientific analysis as they are important to an understanding of family life.

Summary

1. Family life is richly complex, and its study may be approached (a) as an aspect of the life of the larger society, (b) as a psychosocial group, (c) in terms of husband-wife relationship, (d) as the basic social relationship between successive generations, and (e) as a changing social institution.

2. The present study is an original one, based on some four hundred case records. These were obtained from six sources: authors of autobiographies, university students, residents surrounding a social settlement and participating in its activities, residents in a middle-class suburban area, members of the Junior League, and a group of unselected adults.

3. Three techniques were cultivated in the gathering of information through interactive interviews: inconspicuous listen-

ing, inconspicuous observation, and unsuspected recording.

4. Methodology in the scientific study of family behavior must be adapted on the basis of (a) the subject to be studied, (b) the nature of the persons dealt with, (c) their attitude toward the subject studied.

Subject Index

Adams, family, the, 155 ff.
Allowances, family, 125
Attitudes, parental, in ritual, 42
Autobiographies, as source material for study of the family, 210-212; analysis of rituals in, 31-59; kinds of ritual in, 33
Awakening rituals, 112

Bathing rituals, 93
Bathroom procedures, 113
Behavior patterns, transmitted by rituals, 40
Breakfast rituals, 114
Budgeting, family, 125

Case histories, as source material, 212
Child bearing, beginnings of in family cycle, 141
Child conditioning, through family ritual, 64
Class differentials, 105
Class, social, as a concept, 105
Community-provided rituals, 100
Cultural origin, and family ritual, 88

Doing the dishes, 96-97
Dinner rituals, 116
Dressing rituals, 93

Education, changes in, 91
Evening snack, the, 96

Father-child schedules, 101
Family, the, aging, 149; as launching center, 148; current literature on, 3; expectant, 136; preschool, 143; role in continuity of life and culture, 7; with teen agers, 145;
Family accord, 192
Family continuity, and ritual, 7, 86
Family coöperation, and ritual, 82
Family cycle, 135; as conceptual tool, 150; stages of, 136 ff.
Family etiquette, 70
Family integration, 49, 199
Family leisure, 72
Family life, and group adjustment, 81; challenge of, 1-14; process in, 18; trends in, 22-26
Family meal, the, 99
Family ritual, and cultural origin, 88; and family integration, 49-57, 186-203; and family size, 28-29; and the family cycle, 135-153; as an instrument in cultural transmission, 39; as illustration of social origins, 21; attributes of in autobiographies, 35-39; changing extent of, 27-28; characteristics of, 21-26; class differentials in, 105-135; examples of, 18; in autobiographies, 31-59; kinds of, in autobiographies, 33-34; meaning and changing nature of, 14; of the Adams family, 159; secularization of, 26; special power of, 62; three generations of, 154 ff; trends in, 22-26, 90-103

Index of Authors